C FOR PROFESSIONAL PROGRAMMERS
Second Edition

ELLIS HORWOOD SERIES IN COMPUTERS AND THEIR APPLICATIONS

Series Editor: IAN CHIVERS, Senior Analyst, The Computer Centre, King's College, London, and formerly Senior Programmer and Analyst, Imperial College of Science and Technology, University of London

C FOR PROFESSIONAL PROGRAMMERS
Second Edition

KEITH TIZZARD
Head of Department of Mathematical and Operational Research,
University of Exeter

ELLIS HORWOOD
NEW YORK   LONDON   TORONTO   SYDNEY   TOKYO   SINGAPORE

First published in 1992 by
ELLIS HORWOOD LIMITED
Market Cross House, Cooper Street,
Chichester, West Sussex, PO19 1EB, England

A division of
Simon & Schuster International Group
A Paramount Communications Company

Printed and bound in Great Britain
by Redwood Press, Melksham

British Library Cataloguing in Publication Data

A catalogue record for this book is available from the the British Library

ISBN 0–13–116997–1

Library of Congress Cataloging-in-Publication Data

Available from the publishers.

Contents

x   **Contents**

Preface

When the first edition of this book was in preparation, the preliminary draft proposed standard for the C language was issued by the American National Standards Institute (ANSI), although few compilers, at that time, had implemented the new features. The standard now exists and one can reasonably expect any commercial compiler to conform to it. It thus seemed to be time to rewrite my book, incorporating these changes in the language.

It is difficult to say that any one change is the most important but among those that are providing the programmer with more control over his or her program are: function prototypes, the introduction of const for both data values and pointers and the generic pointer type void * . Furthermore, a standard library of functions has been defined together with a comprehensive set of header files which contain all the necessary prototypes and definitions.

In writing this second edition, I have taken full account of these new features. Although I set out simply to modify the original material I found myself rewriting almost all of it. I have preserved the original order but have changed the emphasis of chapter 4 from examining simple data types to considering expressions. Assignment still justifies a chapter of its own since this, together with the concept of an expression statement, still creates problems for newcomers to the language. The section on storage allocation and dynamic data structures has been made into a chapter of its own with examples of linked lists and dynamically sized arrays.

When teaching the language, I find that I cover the blackboard with numerous diagrams particularly when explaining pointers, structures and arrays. The chapters on these topics now contain more extensive diagrams which, I hope, aid an understanding of the text.

There are numerous new programs, many of which are small, being directed at specific parts of the language. When discussing the size of data items and the limits of numerical values, I have chosen to offer programs which illustrate these instead of merely tabulating the facts. I hope that this approach is more acceptable to the reader.

I acknowledge again the valuable help and assistance I continue to gain from my colleague, Raymond Thompson, who has made most helpful comments on drafts of the book. All the programs have been tested on a Macintosh IIci using the MPW C version 3.1 compiler. It is unfortunate that spell checkers on word processors can only be expected to find certain types of error. I am still horrified when my eye catches, at the four or fifth reading, a word such as 'on' in place of 'of'. Needless to say, any errors that remain are my responsibility.

Keith Tizzard
April 1992

Preface to the First Edition

This book is about a language, called C, which has spread in popularity and use in recent years, yet had its origins in the early 1970's. It was designed by Denis Ritchie from an earlier language, B, which itself was developed from the systems language BCPL. It has long been conjectured whether the successor to C would be D (following the alphabet) or P (following the letters of BCPL); however we now know that it has the ingenious name of C++.

In this book I present a description of the language C. Ritchie's purpose was to design a language in which the Unix operating system could be written. It thus had to be capable of 'low-level' activities, producing compact, efficient compiled code while, at the same time, offering the user 'high- level' program and data structures. Its recent popularity outside systems programming demonstrates that it is a general purpose language suitable for a wide range of applications. It has also broken away from its original Unix environment and is used widely on a number of other operating systems. The rapid increase in the number of 16-bit micro computers has brought with it a new generation of programmers wanting to use C.

Its power and simplicity come at a price. The programmer is made responsible for many aspects of the program which other compilers would check. For example, there is no array bound checking. This is not a language for the novice. If you know how to program in some other language, you will soon learn how to make the best use of C. It is a permissive language and so do not get carried away. Remember the adage: "It does not follow that you must do something, simply because the language allows you to do it."

I learned the language about six years ago when, in common with other programmers at that time, I had to rely on the very limited literature available. In the last two to three years, I have lectured to practising programmers and have realised that, although they were competent in some other language, they needed help and advice in appreciating C. This valuable experience has provided a motivation for setting down in print the approach I have developed in the workshop. I have found that assembler programmers take to the ideas of pointers, incrementation and bit manipulation but sometimes find difficulty in taking to the program and data structuring concepts from high-level languages. Cobol programmers are familiar with data structures but encounter difficulty with the general layout of a C program and with the ideas of pointers. Fortran programmers are at home with the general syntax and program layout but their problems frequently arise when confronted with the concepts of pointers and data structures. Pascal programmers appear to have the least difficulty; they do, however, have to take a different view of the ubiquitous semi-colon. All find the uncluttered input and output facilities an attraction. At the lowest level no magic characters, such as newline, are inserted by the system and at the highest, facilities similar to those in Cobol are available.

As the language has spread, there have been difficulties for programmers and compiler writers in what is to be regarded as standard C. There have been few problems with the language itself since it is small and compact. However, part of its attractiveness lies in availability of an accompanying library of functions which includes, amongst other things, all the input and output and string handling capabilities. If these are different from implementation to implementation, portability of programs becomes impossible. Until very recently the language definition has relied upon the reference manual in Kernighan and Ritchie's book, and the contents of the standard library upon the Unix operating system. The reference manual for this subdivides C functions into two parts: the Unix Programmer's Manual, Volume 1, Section 2 lists system calls whilst Section 3 lists 'subroutines'. For many, Section 3 has represented the standard library which one would expect to find on other operating systems. More recently the American National Standards Institute (ANSI) has begun the procedure of drawing up a standard for the language, together with a library of functions. The consultative process which is involved is likely to take another one to two years before the standard is complete. At the time of writing this book, the preliminary draft proposed standard (document X3J11/85-04) is the best guide to what the final standard will contain. I have followed this throughout the book.

About The Book

In writing a book intended for experienced programmers it seemed best to present first a flavour of the language, relying on the reader's general background. Whilst gaining an overview, he or she should not be put off by points of detail which are different from his or her favourite language. Chapter 1 illustrates the language by means of a number of sample programs. On seeing a new language for the first time, one is frequently less concerned about the new features it offers than the way it does some things differently. I have tried to take the reader steadily from what may be familiar to the new ground. Chapters 2 and 3 examine the general structure of a program before the detail of the simple data types, such as integers and characters, is examined in Chapter 4. The whole of the following chapter is devoted to the one topic of assignment. My experience in teaching others is that, although everyone is familiar with the idea of assignment, many find difficulty with it in C. The major problem arises from the fact that here we have assignment expressions and not assignment statements. This does nevertheless lead to power and compactness. After looking at data structures, a whole chapter is devoted to pointers, another area of difficulty for many. Without an adequate command of pointers the full power of C is not realised.

An outline of what you should expect to find in the standard library is presented in Chapter 12 but special attention has been paid to two groups of functions: string handling in Chapter 8 and input/output in Chapter 11. In each of these, precise details of important functions are presented together with illustrations of their use.

Acknowledgements

I must pay special thanks to my colleague Raymond Thompson, with whom I learned the C language. There have been many occasions when we have together tried to clarify our understanding of some finer points. Our perceptions of programming languages are sufficiently different that I have always benefited from his views. I also wish to thank Mike Banahan and his colleagues at The Instruction

Set for allowing me to lecture to practising programmers. It has long been accepted that the best way to learn is to teach; I have certainly learned a great deal in the process. Finally, my thanks to the editor who must have been driven mad by my repeated use of certain grammatical inaccuracies. His comments were helpful and educational. Needless to say, the faults and errors in the final product are my responsibility.

I hope that you enjoy learning C and that my efforts will be of help.

Keith Tizzard
March 1986

1

Introduction

There are always difficulties in deciding the order in which the parts of a language should be presented. The syntactic definition of a language starts with the detailed components such as constants and identifiers, building upwards through types and expressions to statements. If one follows this route, covering one topic thoroughly before progressing to the next, there is a grave danger of losing sight of the overall direction. It is preferable to see each idea in context, an approach which requires us to use parts of the language before they are fully described.

In this chapter we start by looking at a simple program with a view to noting its general shape and layout. Then we examine a number of other programs, again with the purpose of noting general points showing how ideas that you may expect to find are executed. Precise syntactic details will be left until later. In order to do this we rely on your general programming background. We are setting out not to teach programming but to show to programmers how this language may be used.

Program 1.1 reads a sequence of characters which is terminated by a period (.), namely a sentence and counts the number of blanks and other characters.

The first three statements are directives to the pre-processor to include, as indicated, the contents of a header file named, `stdio.h`, and to define what we mean by `blank` and `period`.

The program proper is contained within the braces { } enclosing the lines from `main()` to the end. In here any variables must be declared before the first executable statement. We declare three variables `numberOfBlanks`, `numberOfCharacters` and `aChar`, the first two as integers and the last as a character. C has a tendency to be cryptic, using `int` for integer and `char` for character although the use of type definition, `typedef`, or the pre-processor's `#define` enables you to replace these by your preferred names.

Program 1.1

```
/* to count blanks and other characters in a sentence
   which is terminated by a period  */

#include <stdio.h>

#define blank  ' '
#define period '.'

main()
{
    int     numberOfBlanks;
    int     numberOfCharacters;
    char    aChar;

    numberOfBlanks = 0;
    numberOfCharacters = 0;

    aChar = getchar();
    while(aChar != period)
    {
        if(aChar == blank)
            numberOfBlanks = numberOfBlanks + 1;
        else
            numberOfCharacters = numberOfCharacters + 1;

        aChar = getchar();
    }

    printf("sentence contains %d blanks and %d other characters\n",
        numberOfBlanks, numberOfCharacters);
}
```

Although we have chosen to declare each variable in a statement of its own we could have written :-

```
int     numberOfBlanks, numberOfCharacters;
char    aChar;
```

Where two or more variables of the same type are declared, the order is unimportant. Again we could have written :-

```
int     numberOfBlanks;
char    aChar;
int     numberOfCharacters;
```

The names of variables are made up of letters and digits and the underscore (_) with the first character being a letter. Upper and lower case letters are regarded as different from each other so that `NumberOfBlanks`, `numberOfBlanks`, `NumberOfBlanks` and `NUMBEROFBLANKS` would be different variables. Words such as `while`, `if` and `else` are reserved and cannot be used as the names of variables; an error occurs if you do so.

1.1 Program Layout

The physical layout of the program is unimportant; it is completely free format. Convention leads us to put one statement per line most of the time with blank lines introduced to aid legibility. White space in the form of blanks, tabs and newlines can be placed almost anywhere. Symbols which are made up of two characters such as != (not equal to), == (equal to) or /* (beginning of comment), must not contain white space. Two consecutive names such as int and numberOfBlanks must be separated by at least one space but elsewhere it is entirely optional. For example, the while and the following (may touch or be separated by white space. Program 1.2 repeats program 1.1 in an unlikely but nevertheless legal layout.

Commands to the pre-processor do not enjoy the same freedom of style for layout. Each must appear on a line of its own with the # as the first character.

Program 1.2   (poorly laid out version of Program 1.1)

```
/* to count blanks and other characters in a sentence
   which is terminated by a period  */

#include <stdio.h>

#define blank   ' '
#define period '.'

main()
{                            /* more than one declaration on a line */
    int     numberOfBlanks;   int   numberOfCharacters; char    aChar;

                             /* more than on statement on a line */
    numberOfBlanks = 0;    numberOfCharacters = 0;

    aChar = /* can put comment here */ getchar();
    while(aChar != period){   if(aChar == blank)
        numberOfBlanks =
        numberOfBlanks + 1;
      else
        numberOfCharacters =    /* statement split over many lines */
        numberOfCharacters + 1
        ;
      aChar = getchar();
    }

    printf("sentence contains %d blanks and %d other characters\n",
        numberOfBlanks, numberOfCharacters);
}
```

1.1.1   Comments

Comments are any characters contained between /* and */ and can appear anywhere that white space is allowed :-

```
numberOfCharacters/* a comment here */=/* or here*/ 0 ;
```

is not very helpful but, again, is legal.

1.1.2   Start of Execution

Every program must have a function called main() which is the starting point for execution. It may also contain subprograms, also called functions, which look similar to our function main() albeit with their own names. There is no distinction between procedures or subroutines on the one hand and functions on the other: every subprogram is a function although it may or may not return a value. No matter how many functions we choose to have nor where we choose to place the main() function within the sequence of functions, execution always starts at main(). All functions, including main() can have arguments but when there are none we must include the empty () when calling them.

1.1.3   Semi-colons

Where to place the semi-colons usually creates problems for newcomers. Once a free format for the program is permitted and we are no longer restricted to one statement per line we have to indicate where one statement ends and the next begins. In C the semi-colon is part of certain statements and thus acts as a terminator to them; it is not to be regarded as a statement separator, placed between statements.

Each declaration ends with a semi-colon:-

```
int numberOfBlanks ;
```

Chapter 4, on Expressions, and Chapter 5, on Assignment, explain more fully the rôle of the semi-colon but, for the moment, we can regard assignment as a statement which ends with a semi-colon:-

```
numberOfBlanks = 0 ;
```

Chapter 2 details each statement in the language, noting which ones need a semi-colon. Here, we can notes that the while statement and the if statement do not themselves need a semi-colon but the statements contained within them may do. Hence, in Program 1.1, the semi-colon inside the if statement immediately before the else is part of the assignment statement:-

```
numberOfBlanks = numberOfBlanks + 1 ;
```

A function call is followed by a semi-colon:-

```
printf(...) ;
```

1.2 Simple Input and Output

Input and output statements are not part of the C language, but a library of useful routines is provided (see Chapter 13). The function getchar() obtains the next character from the standard input. There is a complementary function putchar() but we have chosen to use the more general printf(). In this, the first argument is a string setting out the format of the line to be printed; this includes any textual material such as 'sentence contains' together with special format desciptors, such as %d, which state how the following arguments are to be represented. There may be any number of arguments but there should be the same number of format descriptors. In :-

```
printf("sentence contains %d blanks and %d other characters\n",
            numberOfBlanks, numberOfCharacters);
```

the first %d is replaced by the value of numberOfBlanks and the second %d by numberOfCharacters. A possible line produced by this statement is :

```
sentence contains 7 blanks and 32 other characters
```

The character '\n' is C's way of representing the new-line character. It may be an irritation to some that you have to manipulate it in this way but it has the great advantage that in both input and output you know what you are dealing with; the system does no introduce extra characters. We are thus able to permit further output on the same line or to complete it as we wish.

We could have produced the same output by two statement :-

```
printf("sentence contains %d blanks", numberOfBlanks);
printf(" and %d other characters\n", numberOfCharacters);
```

where the first does not contain '\n' thus enabling the second statement to produce its output on the same line.

Input and output statements need some definitions which are contained in a special file. The opening statement:-

```
#include <stdio.h>
```

tells the pre-processor to include the contents of the file stdio.h at this stage.

A program which copies its input to its output is simple and straightforward. We merely obtain each character by the function getchar() and output it by putchar(). Every character whether it is printable, non-printable, a newline or a tab etc. is copied. Program 1.3 will copy any file. C does not introduce or modify characters on input and does not produce extra ones on output.

The constant EOF is defined in the header file stdio.h. It may seem strange that we are storing the value returned by getchar() in a variable, character, which has been defined as int instead of char. getchar() needs to be able to return every possible character value plus one extra to represent EOF. In C characters are simple regarded as small integers.

Program 1.3

```
/* to copy input to output  */

#include <stdio.h>

main()
{
    int character;

    character = getchar();
    while( character != EOF)
    {
        putchar( character);
        character = getchar();
    }
}
```

1.3 Illustrative Programs

Let us assume that a program needs to have input made up of lines, all of the same length, say 80 characters. Program 1.4 prepares input for such a program by converting its own input to equivalent output in which the length of each line is the required 80 characters. Short lines are padded with blanks whereas long lines are truncated. The end of each input line is detected by testing for the character '\n' whilst the end of each output line is formed by outputting '\n'.

Program 1.4

```
/* make all lines up to the same length */

#include <stdio.h>

#define lineLength  80
#define padCharacter ' '

main()
{
    int aChar;                            /* a character read in */
    int nChars;                        /* character count in a line */

    nChars = 0;
    aChar = getchar();
    while( aChar != EOF)
    {
        if( aChar == '\n')                           /* new-line? */
        {                     /* short line needs extra pad characters */
            while( nChars < lineLength)
            {
                putchar(padCharacter);
                nChars = nChars + 1;
            }
            putchar( '\n');               /* complete the output line */
            nChars = 0;                        /* reset for next line */
```

```
        }
        else if(nChars < lineLength)
        {                              /* input character copied to output */
            putchar(aChar);
            nChars = nChars + 1;
        }
        aChar = getchar();                      /* obtain next character */
    }
}
```

1.3.1 Compact Style of Writing Programs

At this stage it should be pointed out that an experienced C programmer would
have written the program in a more compact form. We leave you to compare
Program 1.4 with the following Program 1.5 which performs the identical task.
Until we have introduced the necessary concepts we will write our programs in the
longer manner, but later on we will compress these where appropriate. As with so
many features in languages one can go too far. Some people pride themselves on
producing extremely compact programs. Whilst this practice has some advantages it
can nevertheless lead to unintelligible programs. We try to maintain a balance
between compactness and legibility.

Program 1.5   *compact form of Program 1.4*

```
/* make all lines up to the same length */

#include <stdio.h>

#define lineLength 80
#define padCharacter ' '

main()
{
    int character;
    int nChars = 0;

    while((character = getchar()) != EOF)
    {
        if( character == '\n')
        {
            while( nChars++ < lineLength)
                putchar(padCharacter);
            putchar( '\n');
            nChars = 0;
        }
        else if(nChars++ < lineLength)
            putchar(character);
    }
}
```

1.3.2   Program Arguments

If we want to make all lines in our output to be some length other than 80 characters, we could edit the program source file to change the statement:

```
#define lineLength 80
```

and then recompile and execute the program. One useful feature of C is that it can access arguments given in the command line which causes execution of the program.

Program 1.6

```
/* make all lines up to the same length
   line length set by program argument   */

#include <stdio.h>
#include <stdlib.h>

#define defaultLineLength  80
#define padCharacter         ' '

main(int nArgs, char * argument[])
{
    int character;
    int nChars = 0;
    int lineLength;

    if( nArgs < 2)                          /* set line length to default */
        lineLength = defaultLineLength;
    else                                    /* convert argument to number */
        lineLength = atoi(argument[1]);

    while((character = getchar()) != EOF)
    {
        if( character == '\n')
        {
            while( nChars++ < lineLength)
                putchar( padCharacter);

            putchar( '\n');
            nChars = 0;
        }
        else if (nChars++ < lineLength)
                putchar( character);
    }
}
```

Suppose that our source file which contains the C statements, is called `length.c` and that we want the executable file to be called `length`; we would, under Unix, compile the program by :-

```
cc -o length length.c
```

and then execute it by the command :-

```
length
```

It would be desirable to be able to type :-

```
length 60

length 150
```

to cause lines to be set to some value other than 80 but still to maintain the original form to produce lines of length 80. Progam 1.6 enables us to do just this. The command line is passed to the program as an array of character strings argument which the program can handle as it wishes. The first argument to main(), nArgs, is an integer variable indicating the number of strings provided to the program.

The program first tests how many arguments have been presented and sets a default line length to 80, if necessary. The library function atoi() converts an ASCII string containing digits to an integer.

1.3.3 Arrays

C provides the capability to form arrays of any type of variable in a manner similar to other languages. Program 1.7 selects alphabetic characters from the input and counts the frequency of each letter.

Program 1.7   (counts frequency of letters in input)

```c
#include <stdio.h>
#include <ctype.h>

#define maxLetters 26

main()
{
    int frequency[maxLetters];
    int index;
    int character;
                                /* initialise the array to zeroes */
    for(index=0; index < maxLetters; index++)
        frequency[index] = 0;

    while((character = getchar()) != EOF)
    {
        if(isalpha(character))
        {
            char letter;            /* declaration of local variable */

            letter = tolower(character) - 'a'; /* find array index */
            frequency[letter] = frequency[letter] + 1;
        }
    }
    printf("Letter Frequency\n\n");
    for( index=0; index<maxLetters; index = index + 1)
        printf("    %c    %6d\n", 'a'+index, frequency[index]);
}
```

The library functions isalpha() and tolower() need the header file ctype.h to be included by the pre-processor. An array, frequency, of `maxLetters` (i.e. 26) integers is declared and then individual elements may be accessed, as in `frequency[letter]`.

The language uses four different bracketing symbols: `[ ]` for arrays, `( )` for functions, `{ }` for compound statements and `/* */` for comments.

This program illustrates how arithmetic may be performed on characters. The array subscripts range form 0 to 25 and so `character - 'a'` is used to compute an appropriate index to the array.

1.3.4   Functions

Needless to say a program can be subdivided into sub-programs which are here called functions whether they return a value or not. Program 1.8 again forms a frequency count of the letters in the input steam but this time is sub-divided into the three steps of initialisation, building the frequencies and displaying them.

Program 1.8
_____

```
/* to illustrate the use of arrays
   counts frequency of letters in input */

#include <stdio.h>
#include <ctype.h>

#define maxLetters 26
                                        /* function prototypes */
void initialise(int count[]);
void buildFrequencies(int count[]);
void display(int count[]);

main()
{
   int frequency[maxLetters];

   initialise(frequency);               /* call the functions */
   buildFrequencies(frequency);
   display(frequency);
}

                                        /* function definitions */
void initialise(int count[])
{
   int index;                           /* local variable */

   for( index=0; index<maxLetters; index++)
      count[index] = 0;
}
```

```
    while((aChar=getchar()) != EOF)
        if(isalpha(aChar))
            count[aChar - (isupper(aChar) ? 'A' : 'a')]++ ;
}

void display(int count[])
{
    int index;

    printf("Letter Frequency\n\n");
    for( index=0; index<maxLetters; index++)
        printf("   %c   %6d\n", 'a'+index, count[index]);
}
```

We have allowed ourselves to write in the more compact form once more. Furthermore, instead of converting upper case to lower case before finding the appropriate place in the array, we have measured the distance of aChar from either 'a' or 'A'. The statement:-

```
    count[aChar - (isupper(aChar) ? 'A' : 'a')]++ ;
```

shows how cryptic and compact C can be and is shorthand for:-

```
    {
        int letter;

        if( isupper(aChar)) letter = aChar - 'A';
        else                letter = aChar - 'a';

        count[letter] = count[letter] + 1;
    }
```

1.3.5   Input of Integers

So far we have restricted ourselves to character input, using the library function getchar(), although we have output both characters and integers by means of printf(). This function permits general formatting of output. General input is possible with the function scanf() but before we can use this we need to know about variable arguments to functions which, in turn, requires a knowledge of pointers. Until we are thus equipped we can create our own function which will read a sequence of characters from the input stream and convert them to an integer if that is possible. Program 1.10 presents the function getint() which achieves this.

Program 1.10

```c
/* getint.c -    obtains an integer from stdin
            skips leading white space stops on a non-digit */

#include <stdio.h>
#include <ctype.h>

#define    stoppingValue 999      /* arbitrary value to stop input */

int getint(void);                          /* function prototype */

main()
{
    int    input;

    do                                          /* infinite loop */
    {
        printf("Type an integer: ");
        input = getint();
        printf("You entered:    %d\n", input);
    } while(input != stoppingValue);
}

int getint(void)                           /* function defintion */
{
    int aChar;
    int theNumber;
    int sign = 1;
                                          /* skip leading space */
    while( isspace(aChar = getchar()) && aChar != EOF)
        ;                                 /* empty loop body */

    if(aChar == '-')
    {                                     /* a negative number */
        sign = -1;
        aChar = getchar();                /* get next character */
    }
    else if(aChar == '+')
    {
        sign = 1;
        aChar = getchar();
    }
                              /* not a digit or end of file */
    if(!isdigit(aChar) || aChar == EOF)
        return 0;                         /* no number read */
    else
    {
        theNumber = 0;
        do
            theNumber = 10 * theNumber + aChar - '0';
        while(isdigit(aChar = getchar()));

        ungetc(aChar, stdin);             /* put extra character back */
        return sign * theNumber;
    }
}
```

Sample input(in bold) and output

```
Type an integer: 123
You entered:     123
Type an integer: 3458
You entered:     3458
Type an integer: -126
You entered:     -126
Type an integer: 999
You entered:     999
```

   The function will read characters, skipping over leading white space, accepting a sequence of digits (optionally preceded by a plus or minus sign). Reading will stop at the first non-acceptable character. The function will return the value of the integer which is represented by the sequence of digits.

   A more compact function to read a sequence of digits as an integer is given in Program 1.11. Greater advantage has been taken of the library of functions. First, an array of characters, `buffer`, has been declared and then a complete line is read into this by means of the functions `gets()`. Its contents are converted to an integer by means of the library function `atoi()`.

Program 1.11

```
/* getint.c -   a function to obtain an integer from stdin
                uses existing library functions */

#include <stdio.h>
#include <stdlib.h>

#define    lineMax    200

int getint(void)
{
    char    buffer[lineMax];

    gets(buffer);                        /* read a complete line */
    return atoi(buffer);        /* convert to integer and return */
}
```

2

Program Statements

C has a small but sufficient group of statements; enough to support well structured programming:

selection statements	`if` and `switch`
looping statements	`while, do ... while` and `for`
compound statement	`{ ... }`
expression statements	function call, assignment and null statement
jumping statements	`return, goto, break` and `continue`

Most of hese have direct parallels in other languages. The idea of an expression statement may be new to you; so too, may be the fact that assignment and calling a sub-program are not in themselves statements. The subtle significance of expressions and their role in C is explained in chapters 5 and 6.

2.1 Conditional Statement

Syntax:

    i)   **if(** *expression* **)**   *statement1*

    ii)   **if(** *expression* **)**   *statement1*
           else   *statement2*

If the *expression* is true than *statement1* is executed. In the second form, if the *expression* is false then *statement2* is executed.

  We will shortly say more about the way in which expressions are evaluated. When testing the value of an expression C regards any non-zero value as *true* and zero as *false*. Although any integral expression is permitted it is frequently the case that we wish to make comparisons between two or more quantities using the relational operators <, >, == etc. and the logical operators && (and), || (or) and ! (not). These have been designed to produce the value zero to represent *false* and the value one to represent *true*.

Neither form of the `if` statement includes a semi-colon; `statement1` or `statement2` may or may not have one, depending on what actual statement each one is. Until we have covered a complete discussion about where semi-colons need to be used, we will draw attention to their presence or absence in each statement.

```
if( status != 0) ....
if( status) ...                        /* compact alternative */
if( nArguments < 3) ...
if( count < MaxLines && table[count] != Limit) ...
```

The following program illustrates the second form of the `if` statement in which one of two messages is displayed to indicate whether a character represents a digit or not.

Program 2.1

```
/* to read a stream of characters and
   to report whether each is a digit   */

#include <stdio.h>
#include <ctype.h>

main()
{
    int     aChar;          /* needs to hold any character plus EOF */

    aChar = getchar();              /* read and store a character */
    while(aChar != EOF)             /* test for end of file */
    {
        printf("(%c) has ordinal value %d and is ",aChar,aChar);

        if(aChar>= '0' && aChar<= '9')printf("a digit\n");
        else                         printf("not a digit\n");

        aChar = getchar();  /* read and store another character */
    }

    printf("\n\nend of input encountered\n");
}
```

In this program `printf("a digit\n");` which is an expression statement represents *statement1* and `printf("not a digit\n");`, another expression statement, *statement2*. The semi-colon is part of the expression statement and plays no role in the `if` statement. The && symbol represents the logical and.

2.2 Compound Statement

Syntax:

```
{
    declarations              /* optional */

    statement1
    statement2
    . . .
    statementn
}
```

Program 2.2   modification of Program 2.1

```
/* to read a stream of characters and
   to report the type of each, converting upper and lower case */

#include <stdio.h>
#include <ctype.h>

main()
{
   char    upper;
   int     aChar;

   aChar = getchar();
   while(aChar != EOF)
   {
      printf("(%c) has ordinal value %d and is ",aChar ,aChar);

      if(isdigit(aChar))
         printf("a digit\n");            /* simple statement */
      else if(islower(aChar))
      {                                  /* compound statement */
         upper = aChar-'a' + 'A';
         printf("the lower case of %c\n", upper);
      }
      else if(isupper(aChar))
      {                                  /* compound statement */
         char    lower;                  /* with declaration */

         lower = aChar-'A' + 'a'
         printf("the upper case of %c\n", lower);
      }
      else
         printf("is a special character\n");
      aChar= getchar();
   }
   printf("\n\nend of input encountered\n");
}
```

We noted above that the `if` statement allows only a single statement to be performed when the condition is true and one when it is false. There are numerous occasions when we wish to perform a whole group of statements. Instead of modifying the syntax of the `if` statement, we have available a compound statement whose rôle is to combine such a group of statements into a single statement. This is simply a sequence of statements enclosed in braces or what some call 'curly brackets'. Declarations are optional but, if present, must precede all other statements; any variables declared at this stage exist only within this particular compound statement.

The compound statement includes no semi-colons. The statements within it may or may not, depending on what each one is.

Program 2.2 extends the testing of an input character; it indicates whether the character is a digit and converts upper case characters to lower case and vice versa. Library functions are used to test for upper or lower case; the conversion is computed directly although there are library functions to handle this as well.

2.3 Multiple `if` Statements

This program also demonstrates the use of the `if` statement to create a multi-way branch. In the first `if` statement, the statement following its `else` is another `if` statement. There is thus no need for the language to provide a special `elseif` statement. By permitting the statement after `else` to be any statement we include the possibility of another `if`.

The contents of the compound statement which forms the body of the `while` loop consist of three statements:

```
printf("(%c) has ordinal value %d and is ",aChar ,aChar);
if(isdigit(aChar)) ...
aChar= getchar();
```

The `if` statement itself expands into the following form:

```
if(...) statement1
else   if( ...) statement2
        else   if(...) statement3
               else    statement4
```

The statement which is to be performed when the condition of the `if` statement is true, namely *statement1*, in the original syntax can also be any statement and so can itself be another `if` statement. In this set of circumstances care needs to be taken since there are two forms to the `if` statement. Consider the following:

```
if(condition1) if(condition2) statement1
else statement2
```

Under what conditions is each statement executed? More particularly, with which `if` is the `else` associated? By laying it out differently, we can suggest different meanings to the human eye but not necessarily to the computer:

```
if(condition1)                                          /* layout 1 */
    if(condition2) statement1
else statement2

if(condition1)                                          /* layout 2 */
    if(condition2) statement1
    else statement2

if(condition1)                                          /* layout 3 */
{
    if(condition2) statement1
}
else statement2
```

In this situation, the else is associated with the latest unmatched if. Although layout 1 suggests that *statement2* is executed when *condition1* is false, this is not the case. Layout 2 indicates, visually, what actually happens. When *condition1* is false, nothing happens. When *condition1* is true, *condition2* is considered and then either *statement1* or *statement2* is executed. The apparent meaning of layout 1 is achieved by layout 3 where the second if statement becomes the only statement within the compound statement. As far as the first if statement is concerned, it does not see the second one and so the else is properly associated with the first if.

2.4 Looping Statements

C provides three looping statements: a while loop and two variations, do ... while and for. The important point to note is that they all incorporate a condition for continuing the body of the loop. There is no repeat ... until loop which would include a terminating condition and the for loop is different from that found in other languages in that it also has a condition for continuation.

2.4.1 while Statement

Syntax:
        while(expression **)** statement

If the *expression* is true the *statement* is executed; the *expression* is again evaluated and the process repeats. In many cases, *statement* is a compound statement; whatever it is, it needs to have some means of changing the expression which is to be tested or else the loop would never end. The *expression* needs to be integral; if it evaluates to 0 (zero) it is regarded as false and if non-zero it is regarded as true. Note that there is no semi-colon as part of the while statement itself; the statement which forms its body may have one, depending on what statement it is.

Programs 2.1 and 2.2 each show a while statement and in each case the body of the loop consists of a compound statement. The following program also uses a loop. Its purpose is to read from standard input, copying to standard output only those characters which had not been enclosed in braces { }. It does this by examining each character which is read in and noting, in the variable nBrackets, the excess of the number of left brackets over the number of right brackets. Only when this is zero does an input character get copied to the output.

Program 2.3

```
/*  to take out characters embedded in brackets */

#include <stdio.h>

const int false = 0;
const int true  = 1;

main ()
{
    int     aChar;
    int     nBrackets;
    int     finished;

    nBrackets = 0;                      /* initialise */
     finished  = false;
     while( !finished )
     {
            aChar = getchar();          /* read and store a character */

                    if(aChar == '.')        finished   = true;
                else if(aChar == '{')       nBrackets = nBrackets + 1;
                else if(aChar == '}')       nBrackets = nBrackets - 1;
                else if(nBrackets == 0 )    putchar(aChar);
     }

     putchar('\n');
}
```

2.4.2   do ... while Statement

Syntax:
> **do**
>   *statement*
> **while(** *expression* **);**

The only difference between this and the while loop is that *statement*, the body of the loop, is executed once and then *expression*, namely a condition, is tested to see whether *statement* should be executed again. The while loop has its test before the body of the loop whereas the do ... while loop has its test after the body. It is however most important to remember that in both cases the test is for continuing the loop. Note that this statement requires a semi-colon as part of it.

The following function finds the square root of a number by means of Newton's method. This uses two estimates of the final result, recalculating them until they are sufficiently close together i.e. within a specified tolerance. In the context of the do ... while we continue with the loop whilst the two estimates are further apart than the tolerance.

Since only one statement is permitted between the keywords do and while and we need two statements we must enclose them in { ... } to create a single compound statment.

```
float squareRoot(float aNumber)
{
    const float tolerance = 1e-3;

    float oldGuess;
    float newGuess = aNumber;

    do
    {
        oldGuess = newGuess;
        newGuess = (oldGuess + aNumber/oldGuess)/2;
    } while( abs(oldGuess - newGuess) > tolerance);

    return newGuess;
}
```

2.4.3   for Statement

Syntax:

```
for( expression1; expression2; expression3 )
    statement
```

The three expressions play the following roles:

expression1	initialisation
expression2	continuation condition
expression3	incrementation

The syntax permits any integral expression for the continuation condition but the other two may be any legal expression. This gives more flexibility than is normally needed and provides programmers with an opportunity to write code which is difficult for others to read. The only semi-colons within the for statement separate the expressions.

The for statement is simply a special form of the while statement:

```
expression1;
while(expression2)
{
  statement
  expression3;
}
```

Many programmers new to C find it difficult to remember that the condition in *expression2* represents the reason for continuing and not for terminating. Some possible for statements are:

```
                      /* simple loop over values 0,1,2 ... N-1 */
    for(index = 0; index < N; index = index + 1) ...

                                /* use of incrementing operator */
    for(index = 0; index < N; index++) ...

                                /* non-integral loop variable */
    for(x = 1.2; x < 11.5; x = x + 0.25) ...

                        /* using the addition assignment operator */
    for(x = 1.2; x < 11.5; x += 0.25) ...

                                     /* looping backwards */
    for(k = Max; k > 0; k--) ...      /* use of decrementing operator */

                               /* scanning a linked list */
    for(ptr = list; ptr != NULL; ptr = ptr->next) ...

                       /* a function to compute the value of n! */
    int factorial(int n)
    {
        int    result = 1;
        int    k;

        for(k = 1; k <= n; k++)
            result = result * k;

        return result;
    }
```

Either or both of the intialisation and the incrementation expressions can be omitted which results in either no intialisation and/or no incrementation:

```
    int factorial(int n)
    {
        int    result = 1;
        int    k = 1;              /* initialised with declaration */

        for( ; k <= n; k++)        /* no initialisation in the loop */
            result = result * k;
        return result;
    }

    int factorial(int n)
    {
        int    result = 1;
        int    k ;
        for(k = 1; k <= n;)        /* no incrementation expression */
        {
            result = result * k;
            k++;                   /* incrementation within the loop */
        }
        return result;
    }
```

Omitting both the intialisation and the incrementation would reduce the `for` statement to a `while` statement. What happens if the condition is omitted? Either it is assumed always to be true or always to be false. In fact, the first is the case: if *expression2* is omitted the condition is assumed to be true. An infinite loop can be formed by:

```
for( ; ; ) ...                                /* loop forever */
```

Some other way must be introduced to cause the loop to terminate.

2.5 Expression Statement

Syntax:
```
        expression ;
```

Any expression when followed by a semi-colon becomes classified as a statement and can thus be used anywhere that the syntax requires a statement. The most appropriate expressions to use in this way are those which have side effects such as assignment, incrementation, decrementation and function calls. Note that the semi-colon is an important and integral part of this statement.

   Examples of expression statements include:

```
index = 1;                             /* assignment */
printf("the answer is %d\n", result);  /* function call */
index++;                               /* incrementation */

index + k;                             /* legal but useless */
```

These statements in themselves are not usually a cause for concern. What is puzzling to the new C programmer is the question 'why is assignment, not followed by a semi-colon, treated as an expression?' Interestingly, we have already seen this in use as the first, or initialisation, expression in the `for` statement. We will return to this question when we have examined expressions more fully.

2.5.1   Null Statement

Syntax
```
        ;                       /* a semi-colon on its own */
```

The *expression* in the expression statement is optional giving rise to a statement which consists simply of a semi-colon. In what way can this be useful? There are occasions when all the activity of a loop is carried out in its condition and/or incrementation. For example, given an array of characters, to find the first occurrence of a particular character we could write:

```
int findChar(char aChar, char buffer[], int bufferSize)
{
    int index;

    for(   index =0;
           index < bufferSize && buffer[index] != aChar;
           index++)
        ;                                      /* null statement */

    if( index >= bufferSize) return -1;    /* not found */
    else                     return index;
}
```

It is good practice to put the null statement on a line of its own and to comment it so that it clearly visible.

2.6 Switch Statement

Syntax:
>   **switch(** *expression* **)** *statement*

The *expression* needs to produce an integral value. To be of general use the *statement* would normally be a compound statement; within this, some of its statements can, and usually would, have special case labels:

>   **case** *constant* : *statement*

Furthermore, one of them can act as a default:

>   **default** : *statement*

The switch statement requires no semi-colon. Section 2.3 discussed how a sequence of if statements can be used to construct a multi-way branch. This however provides a more general mechanism than is needed under certain circumstances. There are occasions when a single quantity is tested for equality against a number of alternative values such as in the first three tests of:

```
        if(aChar == '.')      finished  = true;
    else if(aChar == '{')     nBrackets = nBrackets + 1;
    else if(aChar == '}')     nBrackets = nBrackets - 1;
    else if(nBrackets == 0 )  putchar(aChar);
```

This could be rewritten, using a switch statement as:

```
switch (aChar)
{
    case '.' :    finished  = true;
                  break;
    case '{' :    nBrackets = nBrackets + 1;
                  break;
    case '}' :    nBrackets = nBrackets - 1;
                  break;
    default  :    if(nBrackets == 0 )  putchar(aChar);
                  break;
}
```

The `break` statements are needed to prevent the subsequent statements from being executed. The `switch` statement merely offers a list of statements with entry points specified by the `case` labels. After the expression is evaluated, the statement with a `case` label of that value is executed followed by all subsequent ones until a `break` is encountered. There may be any number of statements between a `case` label and the next `break` statement and any statement can have any number of labels. There need not be a `default` label in which case, if the value of the *expression* does not match any of the `case` label values, control passes to the statement following the `switch` statement. If one is included, then it must be the only `default` label. A controlling loop for a simple dialogue with a user could be:

```
int     aChar;

aChar = getchar();
while( aChar != EOF)
{
    switch (aChar)
    {
        case 'w' : case 'W' :   getFileName();    /* fall through */
        case 's' : case 'S' :   saveFile();
                                break;
        case 'r' : case 'R' :   readFile();
                                break;
        case '?' :              help();
                                break;
        default :               printf("unknown option\n");
                                break;
    }
    aChar = getchar();
}
```

2.7 Jumping Statements

Syntax:

> **goto** *label* ;
>
> **break** ;
>
> **continue** ;
>
> **return** ;
>
> **return** *expression* ;

Any statement may be prefixed by a label, the syntax of which is:

> *identifier* : *statement*

The `goto` statement causes an immediate jump to the statement bearing the appropriate label within the same function. Jumping into a different function is not permitted.

One use of the `break` statement has been discussed in Section 2.6 in connection with the `switch` statement where control passes to the point immediately after the `switch` statement. It and the `continue` statement can also be used in the looping statements: `for`, `while` and `do ... while`. For this to take place, the body of the loop needs to be a compound statement within which one or more of the statements is a `break` or a `continue`. In these the `break` statement again causes control to jump to the point immediately <u>after</u> the closing } of the compound statement and the `continue` to the point immediateley <u>before</u> the closing } causing the loop to proceed to its next iteration.

```
aChar = getchar();
while( aChar != EOF)
{
    if( aChar == 'q') break;

    process(aChar);
    ...
}
/* next statement after the break */

for(index = 0; index < N; index++)
{
    if(a[index] < a[index+1] ) continue;

    process(a[index]);
    ...
    /* next statement after continue */
}
```

A break only affects one level of loop and so, when there are nested loops, control does not jump out of all the loops.

```
for( ... )
{
    for( ... )
    {
        if( ... ) break;
        ...
        if( ... ) continue;
        ...
        if( ... ) goto error;
        ...
        /* next statement after continue */
    }
    /* next statement after break */
}

error: ...          /* error recovery */
```

The return statement provides the means of leaving a function and returning to the point from which is was called. It is explained in the next chapter which discusses functions more fully.

3

Functions

In order to facilitate the good design of well structured programs, a language needs to provide ways in which a program can be sub-divided into small, semi-independent parts, or subprograms. The programmer is then able to design each part to perform a limited task and thus to ensure that it carries out this task well. Most languages provide two types of subprogram:

a) functions which compute and return a value

b) subroutines or procedures which carry out some task without returning a specific value

In C this distinction is not made: there are only functions. A function can, but need not, return a value. If it does, that part of the program which calls the function need not use it. The `printf()` function which enables us to display values on standard output returns an integer value but we rarely have need to use it. Functions can have arguments thus enabling the calling part of the program to pass values to the function. They cannot directly pass back values through their arguments; the later discussion of pointers will show how this can be achieved.

3.1 Illustrative Use of Functions

Let us first consider an example and then discuss the mechanisms by which functions are declared, defined and used.

A program is to read a stream of characters from its standard input, to measure the length of each word in that stream and to report how many words are found, together with the length of the longest word. We need to define what we mean by a word; we will use the definition of an identifier in a C program, namely, a sequence of characters starting with a letter and followed by any letters and/or digits. We can thus view the input stream of characters as words separated by gaps over which we need to skip.

If we had available, or could design, the following three functions we could write a short program to achieve that task:

1   to skip over a gap until the next word, returning true if the next character is a letter and false if the end of file is encountered; no arguments are needed:

```
int skipToWord(void);
```

2   to read and count the letters which make up a word, stopping on the first character of a gap, returning the number of characters in the word; no arguments are needed:

```
int    wordLength(void);
```

3   to display the number of words read and the length of the longest word but not returning a value:

```
void printResult(int nWords, int maxLength);
```

The main part of the program can now be written as set out in Program 3.1.

Program 3.1

```
#include <stdio.h>
#include <ctype.h>

const int false = 0;                    /* define some constants */
const int true  = 1;

                                        /* declare the functions */
int     skipToWord(void);
int     wordLength(void);
void    printResult(int nWords,int maxLength);

main()
{
    int maxLength = 0;
    int nWords    = 0;

    while( skipToWord())
    {
        int thisOne;

        thisOne = wordLength();         /* note this length */
        nWords++;                       /* count another word */
        if( thisOne > maxLength)        /* note the largest */
            maxLength = thisOne;
    }
    printResult(nWords, maxLength);     /* print them */
}
```

As long as the three functions are provided, this will work. The logic of the program is concise but clear. The main loop will keep going if the function `skipToWord()` finds the beginning of a word. The loop body then obtains the length of the word and updates the maximum length to date. The functions `skipToWord()` and `wordLength()` work together in that `wordLength()` assumes that it starts its work when about to read the first character of a word; `skipToWord()` ensures that this is the case. When the loop control encounters the end of file, the function to display the results is called.

A function is called by using its name and by providing, in parentheses, the actual values of any arguments that are needed. Note that, even when a function does not have any arguments, the function name must be followed by empty parentheses: `skipToWord()`. It is by this means that C can distinguish between a variable and a function call. A function call is regarded as an expression: `skipToWord()` is the expression which forms the condition of the `while` loop; `wordLenth()` is the expression which forms the right hand side of an assignment; `printResult()` is followed by a semi-colon thus forming an expression statement.

It is good practice to declare functions before they are used. C does not insist on this but provides a means of prototyping them so that the compiler can check that the use is consistent with the definition. In this program

```
int      skipToWord(void);
```

indicates that `skipToWord` is a function that takes no arguments but returns an integer. The function `wordLength()` has a similar interface. On the other hand

```
void     printResult(int nWords,int maxLength);
```

indicates that `printResult` is a function that takes two integer arguments but does not return a value. In a prototype, the identifiers of the arguments are optional but their inclusion does indicate how the arguments are to be used. It could have been written as

```
void     printResult(int ,int);
```

3.2 Writing the Functions

The three functions needed for the program do not exist and so we must write them. We have already decided on the interface between the calling part of the program and each function which has been set out in the prototypes. We now need to write the definition of each function; by this we mean that we need to write the code in the body of the function.

The function `skipToWord()` will read characters from standard input checking to see whether each one is alphabetic and whether the end of file has been reached. We use the function `isalpha()` from the standard library for this. Its declaration is in the standard header file `ctype.h` which is included at the top of the program. Immediately after the loop we need to determine its cause of termination. If we have reached the end of file, we simply return `false` but if we have come across an alphabetic character, we have read one too many. This character really belongs to the function `wordLength()`; we adopt a device of putting this character back onto the input stream, using a function from the standard library, `ungetc()`. The character is then available for the next input command no matter where that may occur in the program.

Our function definition is thus:

```c
int skipToWord(void)
{
    int aChar;

    do
        aChar = getchar();              /* get and store a character */
    while(aChar != EOF && !isalpha(aChar));

    if(aChar == EOF)
        return false;                   /* indicate end of file */
    else
    {
        ungetc(aChar, stdin);           /* put back extra character */
        return true;                    /* indicate that word is found */
    }
}
```

The function `wordLength()` is similar in that it reads consecutive characters, counting them while each one is an alphabetic or a numeric character, using the library function `isalnum()`. Again the loop will stop when one extra character has been read; this is put back with the aid of the function `ungetc()`. Finally we return the computed length.

```c
int wordLength(void)
{
    int aChar;
    int length = 0;                     /* initialise the length */

    aChar=getchar();
    while(isalnum(aChar))               /* is it acceptable? */
    {
        length++;                       /* increase the length count */
        aChar=getchar();
    }

    ungetc(aChar, stdin);               /* put back extra character */
    return length;
}
```

The final function, `printResult()`, simply displays the two values given to it as formal arguments together with some explanatory text.

```
void printResult(int nWords,int maxLength)
{
    printf("%d words were found\n", nWords);
    printf("The longest had %d characters\n", maxLength);
}
```

This does not return a value. When the closing } is encountered, control itself returns to the calling part of the program. We could have included a `return;` statement but the effect would have been the same.

```
void printResult(int nWords,int maxLength)
{
    printf("%d words were found\n", nWords);
    printf("The longest had %d characters\n", maxLength);

    return;
}
```

3.3 Formal Definition

We need to consider three different but related facets: function definition, function declaration or prototype and function use.

3.3.1 Function Definition

The definition of a function consists of a heading and a body which contains the code of the function. This is where we set out the way in which the function carries out its task.

Syntax:
```
type indentifier(formal_arguments) compound_statement
```

where:

type	the type of value returned by the function; this can be any type other than an array or a function; the special type `void` is used to indicate that the function does not return a value
identifier	the name of the function itself
formal_arguments	declaration of local variables which are intialised to the values of the actual arguments when the function is called

Syntax:
```
type identifier, type identifier ...
```

If the type of the function is omitted, `int` is assumed. If its type is specified as `void`, the compiler is able to check that the body of the function does not attempt to return a value. The compound statement which forms the body of the function can contain, like any compound statement, its own local variables which thus exist only within the function.

Within the body of the function, control is passed back to the part of the program which called the function either when the closing bracket, }, or when a return statement is encountered. The return statement has two forms:

```
return ;
```

```
return expression ;
```

The first form is used for functions whose return type is `void`. The compiler is able to check that the correct form is consistent with the type of the function.

3.3.2 Function Declaration or Prototype

A declaration specifies the details of the interface of the function by setting out its return type and the types of its arguments.

Syntax:
```
    type indentifier( formal_arguments );
```
or
```
    type indentifier( type, type, ... );
```

The first form is the same as the function definition with the compound statement replaced by a semi-colon. It is important that all the details of the heading of the definition and this declaration match exactly. To ensure this, it is commonplace for programmers to copy the heading of the function definition to the top of the program - do not forget to append the semi-colon. The identifiers which represent the formal arguments can be omitted giving rise to the second form.

It is also permissible to omit all details of the formal arguments:

```
    type indentifier();
```

which enables the compiler only to check that the return type used is consistent with its definition. No checking takes place on the arguments.

For the function `printResult ()` the three styles would be:

```
void    printResult(int nWords,int maxLength);        /* full */
void    printResult(int ,int );                   /* abbreviated */
void    printResult();                   /* no argument information */
```

3.3.3   Function Use

A function is called by using its name followed, if necessary, by its actual arguments.

Syntax:
```
identifier( expression, expression, ... )
```

where *identifier* is the name of the function which is being called. The number
of actual arguments must equal the number of formal arguments. When the
function is called, each expression is evaluated and becomes the initial value of the
corresponding formal argument. This formal argument is a variable which is local to
the body of the function; if it is changed, the effect is not transmitted to the actual
argument.

In Program 3.1 the three functions are used in the statements:

```
while (skipToWord ())

thisOne = wordLength ();

printResult (nWords, maxLength);
```

4

Expressions

In general, an expression provides a way of computing a value, sometimes but not always, by combining other values with the aid of operators. Simple arithmetic operations of addition, subtraction, multiplication and division are commonplace within most languages. As well as providing these, C has a large number of operators including incrementation, relational operators, logical operators and bitwise manipulation. C also regards array subscripting and assignment as operators which can be used to form expressions. Furthermore, it has some intriguing ones not commonly found in other languages such as the conditional and sequence operators.

4.1 Types

Each variable and constant used in an expression possesses a type which is specified when the variable is declared or by the construction of the constant. The type indicates what range of values a variable is able to hold together with how much memory is needed to store it. C provides four basic types: `char`, `int`, `float` and `double`. The qualifiers `signed` or `unsigned` can be applied to `char` and `int`, the qualifiers `short` or `long` to `int` and `long` to `double`. This gives rise to the following eleven types:

Type	Alternatives
`char`	
`signed char`	
`unsigned char`	
`short`	`signed short, short int, signed short int`
`int`	`signed, signed int`
`unsigned`	`unsigned int`
`long`	`signed long, long int, signed long int`
`unsigned long`	`unsigned long int`
`float`	
`double`	
`long double`	

4.1.1   Declaration of Variables

Each variable needs to be declared before it can be used. The form of the declaration is:

```
type     identifier1, identifier2, .... ;
```

This enables us to declare one or more variables to be of the same type. Possible declarations of variables are thus:

```
char            aLetter;
int             number;
long            bigNumber, anotherBigOne;
unsigned long   positiveBigNumber;
long double     veryLargeNumber;

signed short int littleOne;
```

Program 4.1

```
#include <stdio.h>
#include <limits.h>
#include <float.h>

main()
{
   printf("Size of basic data types:\n\n");
   printf("Type            Bytes\n\n");
   printf("char            %d\n", sizeof(char));
   printf("signed char     %d\n", sizeof(signed char));
   printf("unsigned char   %d\n", sizeof(unsigned char));
   printf("short           %d\n", sizeof(short));
   printf("int             %d\n", sizeof(int));
   printf("unsigned        %d\n", sizeof(unsigned));
   printf("long            %d\n", sizeof(long));
   printf("unsigned long   %d\n", sizeof(unsigned long));
   printf("float           %d\n", sizeof(float));
   printf("double          %d\n", sizeof(double));

   printf("\nRanges of values for integral types:\n\n");
   printf("short       %12d   %12d\n",    SHRT_MIN, SHRT_MAX);
   printf("int         %12d   %12d\n",    INT_MIN,  INT_MAX);
   printf("long        %12d   %12d\n\n", LONG_MIN, LONG_MAX);

   printf("unsigned short %12d   %12u\n", 0,   USHRT_MAX);
   printf("unsigned       %12d   %12u\n", 0,   UINT_MAX);
   printf("unsigned long  %12d   %12lu\n", 0, ULONG_MAX);

   printf("\nRanges of values of float types:\n\n");
   printf("float         %12.7g    %13.7g\n", FLT_MIN, FLT_MAX);
   printf("double        %12.7g    %12.7g\n", DBL_MIN, DBL_MAX);
   printf("long double   %14.7g    %12.7g\n", LDBL_MIN, LDBL_MAX);
}
```

The amount of storage occupied by a particular type is dependent on the architecture of the computer in use, although typically a `char` occupies one byte and `int` uses the natural size of the machine i.e. 16 bit, 32 bit, 64 bit etc.. The operator, `sizeof,` can be used to find out how many bytes are required to store a value of each type. The range of values represented by each type can be found from appropriate constants which are stored in the two header files `limits.h` and `float.h`. Program 4.1 displays a sample of these for a 32 bit computer.

Sample output (Program 4.1)
_____

```
Size of basic data types:

Type              Bytes

char               1
signed char        1
unsigned char      1
short              2
int                4
unsigned           4
long               4
unsigned long      4
float              4
double             8

Ranges of values for integral types:

short                   -32768           32767
int               -2147483648       2147483647
long              -2147483648       2147483647

unsigned short            0            65535
unsigned                  0       4294967295
unsigned long             0       4294967295

Ranges of values of float types:

float        1.175494e-38     3.402823e+38
double       2.225074e-308    1.797693e+308
long double         1e-4926   1.189731e+4932
```
_____

We will consider other types such as arrays, pointers, structures and unions later. One other simple data type which is a form of `int` is considered next.

4.1.2   Enumerative Type

Some applications require variables which are able to take only a limited range of values. For convenience and clarity these values are given names. For example, in a program concerned with playing cards, we may need a variable to represent the suit of a card. The natural values are `club`, `diamond`, `heart` and `spade`. Without any special language facility we might choose some integer values to stand for these. Any values will do since they are to be used only as indicators; let us use 0, 1, 2 and 3. The program could then contain :-

```
int        card;
...
card = 2;
```

This is a poor way of handling the situation since we need to remember what the value 2 stands for. An improvement would be achieved by using the pre-processor to give names to the values :-

```
#define    club      0
#define    diamond   1
#define    heart     2
#define    spade     3

int    card;
...
card = heart;
```

or even, constant integers:

```
const int club      = 0;
const int diamond   = 1;
const int heart     = 2;
const int spade     = 3;

int        card;
...
card = heart;
```

The language offers a more compact way of achieving the same effect. The enumeration type enables us to set down the values which a variable may take without the need for many #define directives :-

```
enum suit {club, diamond, heart, spade};
```

which defines a new type enum suit together with the values it may take; we may then declare variables of this type :-

```
enum suit    card;
```

Take note that the type is enum suit and that the variable is card. We may then have the following :-

```
card = heart;
...
if(card == spade) ...
```

Care must be taken however. This is not a completely new type; it is simply another representation of the type int. The identifiers club, diamond, heart and spade are given the integer values 0, 1, 2 and 3 and all subsequent operations on enumerative types are taken to be integer. If we foolishly write the equivalent of :-

```
card = heart + spade;
```

the variable `card` will be given the value 5 without any complaint from the compiler.

In spite of this limitation the enumerative type can lead to improved legiblity of programs.

4.1.3 Defining New Types - `typedef`

There are times when it is convenient to define a new type, specific to a particular program. In fact, C does not provide a facility to create truly new types but simply a means of giving new names to existing types. By preceding a normal declaration by the keyword `typedef`, the identifier becomes an alternative name for the type instead of being a variable:

```
typedef    float  velocity;
typedef    int    counter;
typedef    enum {false, true} boolean;
typedef    enum {club, diamond, heart, spade} suit;
```

The identifier `velocity` is now an alternate name for the type `float` and can be used to declare variables:

```
velocity   startingSpeed, maxSpeed;
```

Similarly, we can use the other types:

```
counter    index;
suit       card;
boolean    flag, ok;
```

Some programmers prefer to use meaningful names such as `velocity` in place of `float` although no economy of effort is offered, nor is it possible to alter the possible operations for the type. It may be thought unwise to multiply two velocities and so it would be valuable to prevent such and operation for our new type. Sadly, such a restriction is not possible; we simply have an alternative name for `float`.

A slight economy of effort is offered with the enumerative types where we are able to introduce a single name for a type such as `suit` in place of the previous `enum suit`. We can thus ensure that all our types consist of a single word.

A similar situation occurs with structures which are discussed in Chapter 6.

4.2 Constants

The type of a constant is determined by the way in which it is written. Although not a fully exhaustive list, the following examples illustrate the point:

```
integer constants:  3, 123, -5, 364758, 0
double constants:   1.2, -0.5, 37409.123, 0.0004, 12e3, -64.6e-4
character constants:'a', 'T', '3', '>', '.'
```

We can thus see that a sequence of digits, possibly preceded by a minus sign, becomes a constant of type int. If either a decimal point and/or an exponent is included it becomes a double. Constants of type char are single characters enclosed in quote marks.

Variations on these are possible. If the sequence of digits for an integer makes a number which is too large to be stored in an int then it can be a long constant if the implementation provides a greater range for long than int, or if that is not the case then it can be an unsigned long. If we deliberately want a small quantity to be stored as a long int then we can follow the digits with l or L. On a 16 bit computer which allocates 2 bytes for an int and 4 bytes for a long int then 43456 would be long, whereas on the 32 bit computer used in the above illustration it would be an int. On both computers the constant 3142536728 would be unsigned long. The constants 5L and 311 will be stored as long int on either computer. If we want a positive constant to have the type unsigned int instead of simply int, then we can follow is with u or U, e.g. 34u or 578U.

Sometimes we wish to express the constant in octal or hexadecimal form. Although this has no effect on the way in which it is stored, it may be more meaningful in the context of the program being written. A sequence of digits starting with 0 (zero) is taken to be in octal form; of course, the following digits must be in the range 0 to 7. If the constant starts with 0x or 0X (zero followed by the letter x) then it its taken to be in hexadecimal form and the following characters may be 0 to 9 and a to f or A to F. Some examples are thus:

```
octal integers:          05, 011, 036103
hexadecimal integers:    0x4, 0X104f2, 0x6Ca5d
unsigned octal:          05u, 011U, 036103u
unsigned hexadecimal:    0x4u, 0X104f2U, 0x6Ca5du
long octal:              05l, 011L, 036103L
long hexamdecimal:       0x4L, 0X104f2l, 0x6Ca5dL
```

To minimise the possible confusion between the digit 1 and lower case letter l it is advisable to use the upper case L when indicating a long int.

We noted above that constants containing either a decimal point and/or an exponent are of type double. If however we wish a constant to be of type float the we can follow it with f or F. On the other hand, to make it of type long double we can use l or L.

```
float constants:         0.5f,  -12E5f,  3.45e-5F
double constants:        0.5,   -12E5,   3.45e-5
long double constants:   0.5l,  -12E5l,  3.45e-5L
```

Character constants are simple enough although we need a way of representing the quote (') which is used to delimit the character in question as a character in its own right. This is achieved by using and escape character \ (the back-slash): '\''. This now makes \ a character with special meaning and so when we need to represent this as character in its own right we need to escape it: '\\'.

Some other useful characters do not have a printable form; to overcome this problem the following are legal:

```
'\a'    alert - visible or audible
'\b'    backspace
'\f'    form feed
'\n'    new line
'\r'    carriage return
'\t'    horizontal tab
'\v'    vertical tab

'\''    single quote
'\"'    double quote
'\?'    question mark
'\\'    back slash
```

These become particular useful in text strings which are used in output expressions such as `printf()`.

```
"a text constant"
"a text constant with \" inside it"
"tabbed\tcolumn\theadings"
"a constant on\ntwo lines and completing a line\n"
```

4.2.1   Named Constants

It is often regarded as good programming practice to give meaningful names to constants. This not only makes programs more intelligible but enables the programmer to change the value of a quantity which is to remain constant throughout the execution of the program in a consistent way. These are declared in a manner similar to declaring variables but with the `const` qualifier preceding the type and with the provision of the value of the constant after an = sign:

```
const type identifier = aValue ;
```

The following function, to find the square root of a number by Newton's method, needs a tolerance to control the loop. Introducing a constant named `tolerance` makes its meaning clearer.

```
#include <math.h>

float squareRoot(float m)
{
    const float   tolerance = 1e-3;   /* declaration of constant */

    float         oldGuess;           /* declaration of variables */
    float         newGuess = m;

    do
    {
        oldGuess = newGuess;
        newGuess = (oldGuess + m/oldGuess)/2;
    } while(fabs(oldGuess - newGuess) >= tolerance);

    return   newGuess;
}
```

Other examples could be:

```
const char        endOfSentence = '.';
const unsigned    mask          = 0xffff;
```

4.3 Order of Evaluation

We have noted above, that expressions are constructed from constants and variables combined together by operators. Most of these are binary in nature in that they combine two quantities (+ * ...); one group however is unary in that its members operate on only one quantity (! - ...); one particular operator, the conditional operator (? :), is, in fact, ternary in that it combines three quantities.

When an expression contains two or more operators it is necessary to understand the order in which the operations are carried out. For example, we would expect all the following to have the same effect and ultimate value:

```
                                                      /* example 1 */
one * two + three / four
(one * two) + three / four        /* unnecessary parentheses */
one * two + (three / four)        /* unnecessary parentheses */
(one * two) + (three / four)      /* unnecessary parentheses */
```

whereas the following would have a different meaning and effect:

```
one * (two + three) / four                            /* example 2 */
```

If these were float variables containing, respectively, the values 1.0, 2.0, 3.0 and 4.0, example 1 would produce the value 2.75 but the example 2 would produce 2.25.

Furthermore, which of the following are equivalent with respect to the order of evaluation?

```
first * second / third                                /* example 3 */
(first * second) / third
first * (second / third)
```

If these variables were ints containing, respectively, the values 7, 12 and 5 these three expressions would produce the values 16, 16 and 14. Integer division causes truncation.

Two concepts come to our aid: the *precedence* and *associativity* of the operators. Table 4.1 sets out all the C operators in groups with the highest precedence, namely 'postfix', at the top and that with the lowest precedence, namely 'sequence', at the bottom. The associativity within each group is shown to the right of the table. In example 1, we would naturally expect multiplication (*) and division (/) to be carried out before addition (+) and this is, in fact, what happens: the table shows that the multiplicative operators have a higher precedence than the additive operators. The order of precedence can always be changed by the use of parentheses as example 2 shows. Unnecessary parentheses can be used as shown in example 1.

Sometimes this makes the intended meaning clearer but too many can sometimes be counter-productive.

Table 4.1

Group	Operators	Associativity
postfix	() [] . ->	left to right
unary	! ~ ++ -- + - * & (type) sizeof	right to left
multiplicative	* / %	left to right
additive	+ -	left to right
shifting	>> <<	left to right
relational	< <= > >=	left to right
equality	== !=	left to right
bitwise and	&	left to right
bitwise complement	^	left to right
bitwise or	|	left to right
logical and	&&	left to right
logical or	||	left to right
conditional	?:	right to left
assignment	= += -= *= /= %= &= ^= |= <<= >>=	right to left
sequence	,	left to right

When an expression contains two or more operators from the same group, such as in example 3, the order in which they are performed is determined by their associativity which is either from left to right, or vice versa, through the expression. Since the associativity in the multiplicative group is from left to right, the first two lines in example 3 are equivalent but are different from the third line. It needs to be stressed that the left to right order applies to the way in which the operators are written in the expression and not to the way that they appear in the table. Thus the following are equivalent:

```
first / second * third
(first / second ) * third
```

and these are different from:

```
first / (second * third)
```

In summary, the operators are formed into groups. The language specifies a precedence between the groups such that when an expression contains operators from different groups those in the group with the higher precedence are used before those in the lower precedence groups. Where we have a number of operators in the same group the associativity determines whether these operations are performed from left to right or from right to left.

In an expression used to represent a condition for an `if` statement, we frequently need to use a combination of arithmetic operators and relational operators:

```
if(thisOne + thatOne > 20 && n < Max) ...
```

fortunately has the same meaning as:

```
if(((thisOne + thatOne) > 20) && (n < Max)) ...
```

The precedence of the groups of operators shows that the addition is performed first, followed by the relational operators (> <) and finally the logical operator (&&). Pascal programmers would need to use some, but not all, of these sets of parentheses to have the desired effect.

Most the operators that we will consider in this chapter have 'left to right' associativity. Those in the unary and assignment groups will be examined later.

4.4 Arithmetic Operators

Arithmetic binary operations (+ - * / %) work only on a pair of expressions of the same type, although it is permissible to write expressions which mix different types. In the background, conversion from one type to another takes place and although what happens is usually quite natural, it is as well to know the rules followed by the compiler. The types can be regarded as ranging from wide to narrow where a wider type can contain all the values of a narrower one. For example, all the values of int could be contained in a variable of type float. The types, from widest to narrowest, are:

```
long double
double
float
unsigned long
long
unsigned
int
short            (always converted up to int)
unsigned char    (always converted up to int)
signed char      (always converted up to int)
char             (always converted up to int)
```

Note that no computations are performed in short, unsigned char, signed char or char. Any quantity of these types is implicitly converted to int before computation. If the two quantities involved in an operation are then not of the same type, the narrower type is widened to the wider type, which becomes the type of the result. For example:

```
float  result;
float  sum;
int    data;

result = sum + data;
```

data is widened to float so that it is the same type as sum; and the value of the addition is of type float no matter what the type of result is.

Across assignments widening takes place in the same way. That is, if the left hand side is wider than the right hand side, the assignment is straightforward. Should the variable to which a value is being assigned be of narrower type than the type of the expression on the right, loss of precision may occur. Assigning from a wider to a narrower integral type, e.g. from `long` to `int`, will cause the high order bits to be lost. Assigning `double` to `float` will cause rounding or truncation, depending on the implementation; assigning `float` to `int` causes truncation by the loss of the fractional part (although the effect on negative values may be machine dependent).

Passing arguments to functions is similar. With the introduction of function prototypes into the language, actual arguments will be converted to the type of the formal argument. Program 4.2 contains two functions, one of which takes an integer argument and the other a float argument. Each is called with an integer and then a float. Its output confirms that the integer is acceptable to the float argument and that the float is truncated as it is passed to the integer argument.

Program 4.2

```
#include <stdio.h>

void floatFunc(float thing);
void intFunc(int thing);

main()
{
    float   floatObject = 57.6;
    int     intObject   = 13;

    floatFunc(intObject);
    floatFunc(floatObject);

    intFunc(intObject);
    intFunc(floatObject);
}

void floatFunc(float thing)
{
    printf("floatFunc %.2f\n", thing);
}

void intFunc(int thing)
{
    printf("intFunc    %d\n", thing);
}
```

Sample output

```
floatFunc 13.00
floatFunc 57.60
intFunc    13
intFunc    57
```

4.4.1   Integer Operations

Two integers may be combined to produce another integer by using the arithmetic operators :-

```
+       addition
-       subtraction
*       multiplication
/       division
%       remaindering
```

The first three are straightforward. Division of one positive by another integer causes truncation of any potentially fractional part and the remainder operator % yields the smallest possible remainder :-

```
int    numerator    = 33;
int    denominator  =  5;
int    dividend;
int    remainder;

dividend  = numerator / denominator;        /* yields value 6 */
remainder = numerator % denominator;        /* yields value 3 */
```

Remaindering is useful in such constructions as :-

```
if(number % potentialFactor == 0)
    printf("%d is a factor of %d\n", potentialFactor, number);

if(number % 2 != 0)
    printf("%d is odd\n", number);
```

4.4.2   Character Operations

Characters are represented as integers and, as a consequence, are interchangeable with them. Although we can perform any of the integer operations on char it usually makes sense to restrict ourselves to :-

```
char    +    int        yielding    char
char    -    int        yielding    char
char    -    char       yielding    int
```

Multiplying and dividing characters, whilst legal, has little practical meaning. To print the letters of the alphabet together with their ASCII representations:

```
char    aChar;

for(aChar = 'a'; aChar <= 'z'; aChar++)
    printf("%c  %d\n", aChar, aChar);
```

4.4.3   Floating Point Operations

Two expressions of type `float` (or `double`) may be combined by the following operators to yield a `float` (or `double`) result :-

```
+            addition
-            subtraction
*            multiplication
/            division
```

The exponentiation operator, available in some languages, is not provided. To raise an expression to a power it is necessary to use the library function `pow(x, y)` whose prototype is:

```
double  pow(double x, double y);
```

which raises x to the power y and yields a `double` result. The prototype is contained in the header file `<math.h>` which should be included.

4.5   Casting

There are times when we wish to cause a temporary change of type. Here `casting` will be of help. Any expression may be pre-fixed by

```
( type )
```

to change its type to the indicated type.

For example, integer division causes truncation which may not be wanted:

```
int     numerator;
int     denominator;
float   result;

result = numerator / denominator;                    /* truncation */

result = (float)numerator / denominator;        /* no truncation */
result = numerator / (float)denominator;

                                /* no truncation, but overkill */
result = (float)numerator / (float)denominator;
```

The type of `numerator` or `denominator` is not changed permanently but only for the purposes of this calculation.

4.6   Logical and Relational Operations

The language does not provide a logical, or boolean, data type but relational operations `<`, `>`, `==` etc produce values which are convenient to regard as `true` and `false` and statements such as `if` and `while` test them. When producing these results `false` is represented by the integer zero and `true` by 1 (one). When testing a value, zero is regarded as `false` and non-zero as `true` .

Although the language deals in integers it is helpful, when writing programs, to think in terms of boolean quantities. To this end we choose to define our own data type together with values `true` and `false`:

```
typedef  int  boolean ;

const int false  = 0;
const int true   = 1;
```

an alternative is to create an enumerative type:

```
typedef enum {false, true} boolean;
```

Either of these can be incorporated at the heading of a program file or simply placed in a file of their own called `bools.h` (say) which can then be included by :-

```
#include "bools.h"
```

A pair of arithmetic expressions of any type (and later, pointer type) can be compared by any of the six relational operators to yield a `boolean` result. The six are :-

```
>         greater than
>=        greater than or equal to
<         less than
<=        less than or equal to
==        equal to
!=        not equal to
```

Note especially that the operator for testing the equality of two expressions is `==` and not merely `=` which signifies assignment. In many cases where the former is to be used the latter is syntactically acceptable but with a wholly different meaning - so beware! A common error is to write :-

```
if(index = 0) ...
```

but this assigns 0 to `index` and then determines whether the result is non-zero i.e. `true`, or 0 i.e `false` (which of course it is). Boolean expressions themselves may be combined by the boolean operators `&&` and `||` to produce boolean values. Hence new expressions may be formed by:

$$exprA \quad booleanOperator \quad exprB$$

where *booleanOperator* is one of:-

`&&`   produces the value `true` if and only if both its sub-expressions are `true` and `false` if either of them is `false`

`||`   produces the value `true` if either or both its sub-expressions is `true` and `false` if both are `false`

Although these are commutative operations, in that we would normally regard exprA && exprB to be the same as exprB && exprA, it is guaranteed in C that exprA is evaluated before exprB. In fact if the final result can be determined from the value of exprA, exprB is not evaluated. By this we mean that:

&&   if exprA is false exprB is not evaluated

|| if exprA is true exprB is not evaluated

For example, if we were wishing to search an array for a particular value and had to take care not to exceed the dimension of the array, we could safely write:

```
int    list[MAXLIST];
int    index;
int    sought;

index = 0;
while(index < MAXLIST && list[index] != sought)
      index++ ;
```

If the value sought is not in list the final value of index which is tested is MAXLIST. Trying to access list[MAXLIST] could cause trouble, since it is one step beyond the end of the array. Fortunately this is not attempted, because index < MAXLIST produces false which is sufficient for the whole boolean expression to be evaluated as false.

In another situation we may wish to read a character and test whether it is an end of line '\n' or an end of file EOF:

```
if((aChar = getchar()) == '\n' || aChar == EOF) ...
```

Here we are assured that aChar == EOF will not be evaluated before aChar is given a value in the first sub-expression.

One further boolean operation is available; namely the negation of a boolean quantity by means of ! which produces true if it operates on an expression with value false and false if it operates on an expression with value true. For example, if we are measuring the length of an input word which is defined as being terminated by white space, the following might suffice:

```
/*      counts characters up to first white space.
        assumes that it starts on an acceptable character     */
int word_length(void) {
    int ch;
    int n = 0;

    while(!isspace(ch=getchar()))        /* while not white space */
        n++ ;

    ungetc(ch, stdin);
    return(n);
}
```

The function `isspace()` returns `true` or `false` which is then reversed by the `!` operator.

Another example is to skip input until we encounter either an end of line or the end of file:

```
while( !((c = getchar()) == '\n' || c == EOF))
      ;
```

All the parentheses are necessary since we want the negation to take place last. An alternative, of course, is :-

```
while((c=getchar()) != '\n' && c != EOF)
      ;
```

4.7 Bitwise Operations

In addition to the set of arithmetic operators C provides full control of bit patterns with the following operators. The first three take two operands and produce a result in which the individual bits depend on the bits in the corresponding positions of the operands. We indicate when a 1 bit appears in the result; otherwise a 0 bit occurs. For the shifting operators, the second argument must be integral and represents how many bit positions are to be shifted. The operand itself is not altered; the expression produces a result which is a copy of the operand suitably shifted. The complement operator similarly produces a result in which the bits are the opposite of the operand.

Operator	Meaning	Result
&	and	1 if both operands are 1
|	inclusive or	1 if either or both operands are 1
^	exclusive or	1 if either but not both operands are 1
<<	left shift	pattern moved left by second operand
>>	right shift	pattern moved right by second operand
~	complement	1 if operand is 0, 0 if operand is 1

The effect of each of these is best demonstrated by an example. We will use sixteen bit numbers to save space. Program 4.3 sets out the effect of each of the operators.

In the function `printBits()` we need to move the bits in the variable `mask` one to the right. It is thus necessary to put the result of the shifting expression back into `mask`. In the chapter on assignment we will see a more compact way of achieving this.

The condition of the `if` statement needs the additional parentheses. The operator `==` has higher precedence than the operator `&`; without the parentheses the value of `mask` would be compared to zero and then the result of this would be used by the `&` operator. This would be syntactically correct but not what is needed here.

Program 4.3

```c
#include <stdio.h>

void printBits(unsigned short aNumber);
void display(char message[], unsigned short aNumber);

main()
{
    unsigned short first  = 0xfb1e;
    unsigned short second = 0xcedd;

    printf("Expression             binary               decimal");
    printf("    octal      hex\n\n");

    display("first", first);
    putchar('\n');

    display("~ first", ~first);
    display("first << 3", first << 3);
    display("first >> 3", first >> 3);
    putchar('\n');

    display("first", first);
    display("second", second);
    putchar('\n');
    display("first & second", (first & second));
    display("first | second", (first | second));
    display("first ^ second", (first ^ second));
}

void display(char message[], unsigned short aNumber)
{
    printf("%-20s", message);
    printBits(aNumber);
    printf("%9d%8o%8x", aNumber, aNumber, aNumber);
    putchar('\n');
}

void printBits(unsigned short aNumber)
{
    unsigned short mask = 0x8000;

    while(mask > 0)
    {
        if((aNumber & mask) == 0)  putchar('0');
        else                       putchar('1');
        mask = mask >> 1;
    }
}
```

Sample output

Expression	binary	decimal	octal	hex
first	1111101100011110	64286	175436	fb1e
~ first	0000010011100001	1249	2341	4e1
first << 3	1101100011110000	55536	154360	d8f0
first >> 3	0001111101100011	8035	17543	1f63
first	1111101100011110	64286	175436	fb1e
second	1100111011011101	52957	147335	cedd
first & second	1100101000011100	51740	145034	ca1c
first | second	1111111111011111	65503	177737	ffdf
first ^ second	0011010111000011	13763	32703	35c3

One common use of these bit manipulation operators is when we wish to maintain a group of related flags or indicators. Each bit of an `unsigned int` can be used as a specific indicator:

```
#define    lowerCase 1           /* 0000 0000 0000 0001 */
#define    bold      2           /* 0000 0000 0000 0010 */
#define    italic    4           /* 0000 0000 0000 0100 */
#define    underline 8           /* 0000 0000 0000 1000 */

unsigned  flags = 0;

flags = flags | bold;            /* switch on bold */

flags = flags & ~italic;         /* switch off italic */

if((flags & underline) == underline) .../* test for underline */

if(flags & underline ) ...       /* test for underline */
```

4.8 Conditional Operator

In the function `printBits()`, we output either `'0'` or `'1'`, depending on the outcome of a test condition. Instead of an `if` statement we could have used a *conditional expression*:

```
putchar((aNumber & mask) == 0 ? '0': '1');
```

Here, the argument of the function `putchar()` is dependent on the result of the condition. The function, `printBits()`, would now look like:

```
void printBits(unsigned short aNumber)
{
    unsigned short mask = 0x8000;

    while(mask > 0)
    {
        putchar((aNumber & mask) == 0 ? '0': '1');
        mask = mask >> 1;
    }
}
```

The general form of the conditional expression is:

expression1 **?** *expression2* **:** *expression3*

in which the value of the whole expression is either *expression2* or *expression3* according to whether *expression1* is true or not. Since a call to a function is itself an expression we could also have written:

```
(aNumber & mask) == 0 ? putchar('0'): putchar('1');
```

In printing some results we may wish a message to read:

```
Length = 1 metre
```

instead of the commonly discovered:

```
Length = 1 metres
```

where the programmer chose not to handle the possibility of the singular. This may be accomplished by:

```
printf("Length = %d metre%c\n", n, n==1 ? '' : 's');
```

where the character printed after metre is nothing at all or else s.

4.9 Sequence Operator

A new expression may be formed from a sequence of other expressions by separating them by , . The expressions in the sequence are evaluated from left to right and the value of the whole expression is that of the right-most one in the sequence.

Example: a palindrome is a string of characters which reads the same backwards as it does forwards. A function to test whether a given string is palindromic needs a for loop with two indices, one moving from left to right and another moving the other way. Both need to be initialized and incremented.

Program Extract   (tests whether the string message is palindromic)

```
#include <string.h>
typedef    enum {false, true} boolean;

boolean ispal(char message[])
{
    int    left;
    int    right;
    boolean ok_sofar = TRUE;

    for(  left = 0, right = strlen(message) -1;   /* initiliase both */
        left < right && ok_sofar;
        left++, right--)              /* increment/decrement both */
        ok_sofar = (message[left] == message[right]);

    return ok_sofar;
}
```

The syntax of the `for` statement, namely :-

    for(*expression1* ;*expression2* ;*expression3*) *statement*

is preserved but each of *expression1* and *expression3* is a sequence of two expressions separated by commas. *expression1* is made up of the two expressions: `left = 0` and `right = strlen(message) -1`. Linking them together with the aid of the comma operator simply creates a new expression which the syntax of the `for` statement accepts.

Another use is where we have a sloop in which we prompt the user for some input where we are able to include the prompt within the condition of the while statement:

```
while(printf("Enter a value: "), gets(buffer) != NULL)
    process(buffer);
```

The expression which makes up the condition consists of two expressions, separated by a comma operator. The value of the `printf()` expression is not used but the value of the complete expression is the value of the `!=` test and it is this that determines whether the loop should continue.

5

Assignment

We have noted, in the last chapter, that assignment is one of the rich collection of operators in the language. In fact there are eleven variants of straightforward assignment in addition to operators for incrementation and decrementation.

Most programmers are familiar with the concept of assignment; it is the common way in which a variable is given a value. The usual situation is that a language has, within its armoury, an *assignment statement*. The problem for newcomers to C is that this language regards assignment as an *expression*. This means that we need to pay particular attention to the rôles of expressions and statements. Chapter 2 discussed the statements of the language which included selection statements such as `if`, compound statement and looping statements such as `while`. The important one, from the point of assignment, is the *expression statement* in which any expression, followed by a semi-colon, is regarded as a statement and can thus be used anywhere that it is legal to have a statement. It is this use of the expression statement that newcomers compare with their assignment statement. It should be noted however that assignment also frequently occurs as the first expression in a `for` statement.

5.1 Assignment Expression

We are familiar with the idea that the purpose of an expression is to compute a value and that the purpose of assignment is to give a value to a variable. Why should assignment be regarded as an operator, along with addition and multiplication, and thus be part of an expression? Look at the following and, in spite of what we have been saying, does your instinct tell you that it is an expression or a statement:

```
result = thisOne + sqrt (thatOne) * something
```

Of course, from what we have said, this is an *expression* and the following is an *expression statement*:

```
result = thisOne + sqrt(thatOne) * something;
```

Not surprisingly, assignment expressions can be used wherever the language permits an expression, such as in the condition of an `if` statement or within the parentheses of a `for` statement; and statements can be used in places such as compound statements or before and after `else` in an `if` ... `else` statement.

An expression is simply a sequence of operators and operands that produces a value and which may, in addition, carry out some other action. An arithmetic expression such as:

```
(fahrenheit - 32) * 5 / 9
```

simply produces a value which may be:

- assigned to variable   `centigrade = (fahrenheit - 32)*5/9`
- passed as argument to function   `centigradeOf((fahrenheit - 32)*5/9)`
- as part of another expression   `100 - (fahrenheit - 32)*5/9`

A logical expression such as:

```
index < Max
```

can be used as a condition to be tested in addition to these three ways:

- test condition   `if(index < Max) ...`
- assigned to variable   `condition = index < Max`
- passed as argument to function   `conditionalPrint(index < Max)`
- as part of another expression   `index < Max && ! finished`

These two expressions simply compute a value without carrying out any other action; they could only do so if they contained a call to a function which itself produced some side effect.

When we regard assignment as an expression we mean that it can be used in any of these four ways. As we can see, an expression produces a value, so what value does an assignment expression produce? The only reasonable choice is the value which is assigned to the variable on the left of the assignment operator. The most common use of an assignment expression is in an expression statement where the value of the assignment is not used!

```
centigrade = (fahrenheit - 32)*5/9;
```

The variable `centigrade` is given a value but the value of the assignment itself is not used. How could it be used? In any of the above ways:

```
if(condition = index < Max) ...
```

```
conditionalPrint(condition = index < Max)
```

In the first, the result of the inequality is determined and assigned to the variable `condition`; its value then becomes the value of the complete expression which, in turn, is used by the `if` statement. An alternative but longer approach which is all that can be performed in some languages, is to carry out two distinct stages:

```
condition = index < Max;
if(condition) ...
```

In the more compact form, the expression `condition = index < Max` contains two operators. Fortunately the precedence of the assignment operator is lower than the inequality which means that the expression to the right of the assignment is carried out before the assignment itself, which is what we would want. In some earlier programs we had the loop construction:

```
aChar = getchar();
while(aChar != EOF)
{
    process(aChar);
    aChar = getchar();
}
```

We need to obtain a character from the input stream at the bottom of the loop so that it can be tested before entering the loop again. To make it work properly on the first occasion, we need to obtain a character once before the loop. A compact alternative is to say *while the character, which I obtain and store in* aChar, *is not the end of file character, process it:*

```
while((aChar = getchar()) != EOF)
{
    process(aChar);
}
```

Being observant, you will have noticed that an extra pair of parentheses has been introduced. This is because the precedence of `!=` is higher than that of assignment. On this occasion, we wish to obtain the character with the library function, `getchar()`, and then assign it to `aChar` before comparing its value with `EOF`. Had we written:

```
while(aChar = getchar() != EOF)                 /* missing parentheses */
{
    process(aChar);
}
```

we would have obtained the character, compared it with `EOF`, assigned the result, either 0 (false) or 1 (true) to `aChar` and then tried to have processed a character with ASCII value 1.

Using this idea, we can write a Program 5.1 to read characters, skipping leading white space and then measuring the length of a word i.e. the number of characters until a blank occurs.

Program 5.1

```
/* to skip white space and then to find the length of a word */

#include <stdio.h>
#include <ctype.h>

main()
{
    int     aChar;
    int     length;
                                    /* skipping leading white space */
    while(isspace(aChar = getchar()))
        ;                                       /* no loop body */

    for(length = 1; (aChar = getchar()) != ' ' ; length = length + 1)
        ;                                       /* no loop body */

    printf("Number of characters: %d\n", length);
}
```

In this program, we see four uses of the assignment operator. Two uses are in ordinary places: the initialisation and the incrementation of the `for` loop. The other two uses are less usual: the first is within the actual argument of the call to the library function `isspace()` which itself forms the condition for the `while` statement. The second is part of the continuation condition of the `for` statement. In both loops, this compaction has led to the loop body being empty. Care needs to be taken under these circumstances because the null statement represented by the semi-colon can get lost to the eye. It is good practice to emphasise in the way in which we have done by placing it on a line of its own. If it were omitted, the next statement would become the loop body; for example, if the semi-colon after the `while` statement had been omitted the `for` statement would have become the body of the `while` statement. The program would have compiled without error but the logic would have been incorrect.

5.1.1 Assignment or Equality?

A common problem which all programmers new to C have to face is the potential confusion between the assignment operator = and the equality operator ==. This frequently occurs in situations such as:

```
result = 13;                         /* or some other calculation */
...
if(result = 0)
    printf("result is zero\n");
else
    printf("result is %d\n", result);
```

which surprisingly produces:

```
result is 0
```

Instead of testing the value of `result` against 0 we have assigned 0 to `result`, losing the value of `13`. The value of the assignment expression itself is now zero which is regarded as false by the `if` statement which, in turn, leads to the statement after `else`. Clearly what was intended was:

```
if(result == 0) ...
```

Some programmers suggest reversing the two quantities being tested:

```
if(0 == result) ...
```

since this is legal for the comparison but illegal if the assignment is erroneously used:

```
if(0 = result) ...
```

This works because the left hand side is not a quantity to which one can legally assign a value. Of course, if the test were something like:

```
if(thisOne == thatOne) ...
```

this approach would not work. In any case, it is not a method that we adopt. It is better to be fully aware of this feature of C and to be ever vigilant. Some compilers do in fact issue a helpful warning.

On balance the advantages of having assignment as an expression instead of as a statement outweigh this one irritation.

5.2 Multiple Assignment

We have seen how assignment can be part of another expression enabling it to appear is unusual places. One use of an expression that we noted was in assigning its value to a variable.

- assigned to variable   `centigrade = (fahrenheit - 32)*5/9`

If we assign the value of an assignment expression to another variable we simply have multiple assignment without the need for the language to make any special provision:

```
temperature = centigrade = (fahrenheit - 32)*5/9
```

In this expression we have five operators and a pair of parentheses. The order of evaluation is as follows:

1   the parentheses come first, causing the subtraction to take place

2   multiplication and division have the next highest precedence with left to right associativity, causing the multiplication to take place before the division

3   this leaves the two assignments whose associativity is from right to left; thus `centigrade` is given a value which becomes the value of that expression and this is assigned to `temperature`.

Multiple assignment works because the assignment operator has a very low precedence and associates from right to left instead of the more usual left to right. Only the sequence operator has even lower precedence. Some programmers take advantage of this in the following construction in which two values need to be exchanged:

```
int     first;
int     second;
int     temp;

if (outOfOrder)
{
    temp   = first;                          /* three statements */
    first  = second;
    second = temp;
}

/* alternative form */

if (outOfOrder)                              /* three expressions */
    temp = first, first = second, second = temp;
```

Some people argue that since the three assignments form a logical group then the second arrangement is to be preferred but it is really a matter of taste. C allows you to express yourself in whichever way you choose.

5.3 Incremental Operators

In parts of programs that count something or scan arrays, we frequently have need to increase the value of a variable by one such as:

```
for (length = 1; (aChar = getchar()) != ' ' ; length = length + 1)
    ;                                        /* no loop body */
```

When we first learnt to program, we struggled with the construct length = length+1 since it conflicted with our mathematical ideas which seemed to suggest that length is equal to length+1. Once we realised that we could change the value of a variable in this way, we were on route to understanding some of the oddities of computer programming. What we were really trying to do was to increment the value of a variable. C offers a direct way of doing this with the incrementing operator ++ :

```
for (length = 1; (aChar = getchar()) != ' ' ; length++)
    ;                                        /* no loop body */
```

This could have been written as a while loop with the incrementation within the body of the loop:

```
length = 1;
while(aChar = getchar()) != ' ' )
    length++;
```

5.3.1 Prefix and Postfix Incrementation

The ++ operator comes in two varieties. It can either precede or follow the variable on which it is to work. Each of the above loops could have been written as:

```
for(length = 1; (aChar = getchar()) != ' ' ; ++length)
    ;                                          /* no loop body */


length = 1;
while(aChar = getchar()) != ' ' )
    ++length;
```

In these particular cases, the effect would have been the same. Which way you write it is merely a matter of choice. There is however a difference between the prefix and postfix forms if there are other operators in the same expression:

```
while(index++ < Max) ...            /* postfix incrementation */

while(++index < Max) ...            /* prefix incrementation */
```

The table of precedence and associativity tells us that ++ has a higher precedence than <. This means that ++ operates on index rather than on the result of the < (if that were to make any sense) but the two forms of the operator do have a different effect. Once it has been determined that ++ operates on index, the timing of its work is delayed in the case of the postfix form until *after* the value of the variable which it is to increment has been used. In the case of the prefix form, it carries out its work *before* the value of the variable is used. This means that in:

```
while(index++ < Max) ...            /* postfix incrementation */
```

the value of index is compared with that of Max, then index is incremented but the value of the whole expression is the result of the comparison, namely true or false. In contrast:

```
while(++index < Max) ...            /* prefix incrementation */
```

index is incremented, then the *new* value of index is compared with Max and the value of this comparison is the value of the complete expression. In each case, if the body of the while loop used the variable index, it would be the newly incremented value. The timing of the incrementation is only relative to other operators in the same expression.

A piece of code that would read characters from the input stream, storing them in a character array but taking care not to exceed the bounds of that array would be:

```
char    answer[Max];
int     aChar;
int     index;

index = 0;
while((aChar = getchar()) != '\n')
    if(index < Max)
        answer[index++] = aChar;
```

The expression `answer[index++] = aChar` contains three operators, in decreasing order of precedence: subscripting `[]`, incrementation `++` and assignment `=`. The effect of the incrementation being a postfix operator means that, although it operates on `index`, its effect is delayed until after the element of the array has been selected. The same value of `index` is used in both the `if` test and this selection; it is then increased, ready for the next time around the loop. The longer way of writing the if statement would have been:

```
if(index < Max)
{
    answer[index] = aChar;
    index = index + 1;
}
```

A different meaning would have been resulted from the following two equivalents:

```
if(index < Max -1 )                        /* long form */
{
    index = index + 1;
    answer[index] = aChar;
}
```

```
if(index < Max -1 )                        /* equivalent short form */
    answer[++index] = aChar;
```

The following fragment illustrates the essential features:

```
int     table[10];
int     index;

index          = 5;
table[index++] = 39;

printf("index: %d table[5]: %d\n", index, table[5]);

index          = 5;
table[++index] = 39;
printf("index: %d table[6]: %d\n", index, table[6];
```

and produces the output:

```
index: 6        table[5]: 39
index: 6        table[6]: 39
```

In each case, `index` has been incremented to 6. In the first case, with incrementation after use, element 5 of `table` has been set to 39; whereas, in the second case, with incrementation before use, element 6 has been set to 39.

5.4 Decrementation

Equivalent to incrementing but changing the underlying variable in the opposite direction is the decrementation operator -- which exists in both prefix and postfix form. Apart from this detail, all that has been said about incrementation applies equally to decrementation.

There are no equivalent operators for multiplication and division!

5.5 Compound Assignment Operators

The incrementation and decrementation operators are very useful but only change the variable concerned by one unit. Sometimes we wish to change it by a different amount. For example, we may want a loop to go up in steps of 3:

```
for(index = 0; index < N; index = index + 3) ...
```

Here, another variation of assignment is of help:

```
for(index = 0; index < N; index += 3) ...
```

True to form, C does not stop there but offers a compound assignment operator for each of the basic arithmetic and bit manipulation operators:

```
+=      -=      *=      /=      %=      <<=     >>=     &=      ^=      |=
```

An expression of the form:

```
variable operator= expression
```

is an abbreviation for:

```
variable = variable operator expression
```

where *operator* is one of + - * / % << >> & ^ | .

Program 5.2 finds the mean value of a set of values read from the input stream.

In the `while` loop of the main program, the number of values is incremented by one but the total is incremented by the latest data value.

Program 5.2

```
#include <stdio.h>

int    getint();

main()
{
    int    data;
    int    nValues   = 0;
    int    total  = 0;

    while((data = getint()) != EOF)
    {
        nValues++;                                      /* increment */
        total += data;                           /* add on the data */
    }

    printf("total               %6d\n", total);
    printf("number of values    %6d\n", nValues);
    printf("average             %9.2f\n", (float)total/nValues);
}

int getint()
{
    char    buffer[BUFSIZ];            /* BUFSIZ defined in stdio.h */

    if(gets(buffer) == NULL) return EOF;
    else                    return atoi(buffer);
}
```

In section 4.6 we discussed the bit manipulation operators. The function printBits() needed to shift the bits of the variable mask one to the right with:

```
mask = mask >> 1;
```

This can now be wrtten as:

```
mask >>= 1;
```

We also discussed switching bit flags on and off with:

```
flags = flags | bold;                /* switch on bold */

flags = flags & ^italic;             /* switch off italic */
```

A more compact form would be:

```
flags |= bold;                       /* switch on bold */

flags &= ^italic;                    /* switch off italic */
```

5.6 Sample Programs

Program 5.3 reads any text file, as its standard input, and replaces consecutive sequences of blank characters by tab characters. The tab size has been set by a defined constant as 8 character positions. The position on the current output line is noted, pos, together with the number of blanks which need to be output, nBlanks, and the number of blanks needed to move to the next tab position, nextTab. The value of nextTab is determined in the condition of the outer while loop. Inside that loop, nBlanks and pos are decremented and incremented, respectively by the value of nextTab.

Program 5.3   (to replace spaces by appropriate number of tabs)

```
#include <stdio.h>

#define      TABSIZE      8
#define      BLANK        ' '
#define      NEWLINE      '\n'
#define      TAB          '\t'

main()
{
    int    inChar ;                     /* input character */
    int    pos = 0 ;                    /* current position in line */
    int    nextTab ;                    /* blanks to next tab */
    int    nBlanks = 0;                 /* blanks left to be output */

    while((inChar = getchar()) != EOF)
    {
        if(inChar == BLANK)
            nBlanks++ ;
        else
        {
            while((nextTab = TABSIZE - pos % TABSIZE) <= nBlanks)
            {
                putchar(TAB);
                nBlanks -= nextTab ;    /* fewer blanks to output */
                pos += nextTab ;        /* move current position */
            }
            while(nBlanks > 0 )         /* output residual blanks */
            {
                putchar( BLANK);
                nBlanks -- ;
                pos++ ;
            }
            putchar(inChar) ;           /* output a real character */
            if(inChar == NEWLINE)       /* reset for new line */
                pos = 0 ;
            else
                pos++ ;
        }
    }
}
```

Program 5.4 accepts a time as an integer, representing the 24 hour clock and redisplays it in an approximate form. It is fun to use a computer to make things less precise! The number of minutes after a five minute interval is determined, rem. A switch statement is used to display an appropriate start to the output such as just after ... . A combination of compound assignment operators is needed to adjust the minutes and hour. The rest is predominantly a multi-way switch using if ... else if ... else ... .

Program 5.4   (to display the time in approximate form)

```
#include <stdio.h>
#include <stdlib.h>

void    approxTime(int hours, int minutes) ;
int     getint(void) ;
void    printHour(int hour) ;

main()
{
    int     time ;

    while( printf("Time ? "), (time = getint()) >= 0)
        approxTime( time / 100 % 24 , time % 100) ;
}




/* ---------------------------------------------------------------
to read a line from standard input and to return it as an integer
--------------------------------------------------------------- */
int getint(void)
{
    char    line[ BUFSIZ] ;

    return atoi(gets(line));
}




/* ---------------------------------------------------------------
to display the hour in acceptable form
--------------------------------------------------------------- */
void    printHour(int hour)
{
    if( hour == 0 || hour == 12)
        printf("12");
    else
        printf("%d", hour % 12) ;
}
```

```
/* ---------------------------------------------------------------
void approxTime ()to display the time in approximate form
----------------------------------------------------------------- */
void   approxTime(int hours, int minutes)
{
   int     rem ;                  /* the minutes after a multiple of 5 */

   rem = minutes % 5 ;
   switch (rem)
   {
   case 1 :
   case 2 : printf("just after ");
            minutes -= rem ;      /* adjust to nearest 5 below */
            break ;
   case 3 :
   case 4 : printf("almost ");
            minutes += (5 - rem) ;/* adjust to nearest 5 above */
            hours += (minutes / 60) ;/* increase hour if 60 mins */
            hours %= 24 ;         /* put in range 0 to 23 */
            minutes %= 60 ;       /* put in range 0 to 59 */
            break ;
   }
                                  /* print the minutes first */
   if( minutes == 0)              /* on the hour */
   {
      if( hours == 0 )
         printf("12 midnight\n");
      else if( hours == 12)
         printf("12 noon\n");
      else
         printf("%d o'clock\n", hours % 12 );
   }
   else
   {
      if( minutes == 30)          /* on the half or quarter hour */
         printf("half past ") ;
      else if( minutes == 15)
         printf("quarter past ") ;
      else if( minutes == 45)
      {
         printf("quarter to ");
         hours = hours<12 ? hours + 1 : 1;
      }
      else if( minutes < 30)      /* before the half hour */
         printf("%d past ", minutes) ;
      else
      {
         printf("%d to ", 60 - minutes);
         hours = hours<12 ? hours + 1 : 1;
      }
      printHour( hours);          /* finally, print the hour */
      putchar('\n');
   }
}
```

Sample input(in bold) and output

```
Time ? 0905
5 past 9
Time ? 1302
just after 1 o'clock
Time ? 1628
almost half past 4
Time ? 1859
almost 7 o'clock
Time ? 0
```

6

Structured Data Types

C provides three ways of grouping the basic data types into useful structures which aid programming :-

arrays   fixed sized groups in which all the elements of a group are of the same type

structures   fixed sized groups of dissimilar types

unions   an overlap of different structures.

Each of these is declared to be of a given size so that the compiler may allocate appropriate memory. The size cannot be altered during the execution of the program.

The chapter on Pointers sets out ways in which arrays whose size is determined at run time can be created and dynamic structures such as lists and trees can be formed.

6.1 Arrays

We will look at a number of aspects of using arrays by considering an example. Characters are to be read from the input stream; a frequency count is to be built up of the letters of the alphabet, ignoring the case of each letter and ignoring characters which are not alphabetic.

We will need an integer array, frequency, of 26 elements so that the frequency of the letter A can be placed in the first element through to the frequency of Z in the 26th element. The array will need to be intialised to zeroes before we start. The characters from the input stream will be read in; for each one that is a letter of the alphabet, its position in the array needs to be determined and then the frequency at that location needs to be incremented. Finally the contents of the array need to be printed.

6.1.1   Declaring Arrays

Syntax:

```
type    identifier[dimension];
```

This declares the *identifier* to be an array of size *dimension*, the elements of which are of the given *type*. The elements can be of any type, those we have already met and those such as structures and pointers which we are yet to meet. The *dimension* must be an integer constant.

Example:

```
int  frequency[26];
```

Since the size of the array will most likely be used in a number of parts of the program it is good practice to give it a name. If, at a later stage, we wish to change the size of the array, we need only change one thing. The pre-processor is useful here:

```
#define   alphabetSize 26                    /* no semi-colon! */

int    frequency[alphabetSize];
```

This declares the variable frequency and allocates space for the 26 integers. Each element can be accessed by use of a subscript, or index, which ranges from 0 to 25. C makes no provision for index ranges other than this.

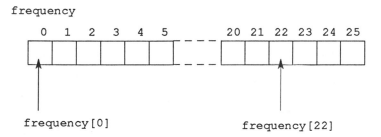

You, the programmer, are responsible for not accessing elements outside the bounds of the array. No array bound checking is provided by the compiler. Errors of this type can be difficult to find since if you overwrite a location outside the array, the problem may not occur until later in the execution of the program.

Simple quantities and arrays of the same type can be declared in the same statement:

```
float  aVariable, anArray[size];

short  anotherArray[bigSize], anotherVariable, moreArray[smallSize];
```

Note that the dimension only applies to the identifier immediately preceding it and not, in the first example, to both identifiers.

6.1.2   Use of `typedef`

It is always possible to define a new array type:

```
                                        /* declare some new types */
    typedef    int     integerArray[size];
    typedef    float   floatArray[largeSize];

                                  /* declare variables of the new types */
    integerArray  myArray, myOtherArray;
    int           aVariable;
    floatArray    vector;
    float         floatVariable;
```

If we choose this approach, all the identifiers in one declaration are of the same array type. The arrays can be used and accessed in exactly the same way as before. It is simply a convenient alternative for declarations.

6.1.3   Accessing Array Elements

Individual elements of an array can be accessed by the `[]` operator. The name of the array is followed by an integer expression contained in `[]`.

- using an array element

```
something = frequency[5]
something = frequency[index]
something = frequency[index+3]
```

- assigning to an element

```
frequency[index] = aValue
```

- element as function argument

```
process(frequency[index])
```

An element of an array can be used in any way that quantities of its type can be used, i.e. you can use the elements of a `float` array in the same way that you can use individual `float` quantities.

A common activity is to scan an array. The `for` statement comes into its own in this context. We need an integer variable to act as an index:

- declare the index

```
int     index;
```

- initialise the index

```
index = 0
```

- increment the index

```
index++
```

- condition for continuing

```
index < alphabetSize
```

- process the element

```
frequency[index] = 0
```

putting these together, we can initialise the array of frequencies to zero:

```
#define    alphabetSize 26

int    frequency[alphabetSize];
int    index;

for(index = 0; index < alphabetSize; index++)
    frequency[index] = 0;
```

Once we have computed the frequencies, we can use a similar statement to print the table:

```
for(index = 0; index < alphabetSize; index++)
    printf("  %c    %6d\n", 'a' + index, frequency[index]);
```

It is most important to remember that the condition of the for statement is one of continuation and that the highest index of the array is one less than its dimension. It is therefore natural to express the continuing condition as *the index being less than the dimension*.

Putting these ideas together, we are able to write the complete program which is shown as Program 6.1

Program 6.1

```
/* to count the frequency of alphabetic letters in the input stream
*/

#include <stdio.h>
#include <ctype.h>

#define    alphabetSize 26

main()
{
    int    frequency[alphabetSize];
    int    index;
    int    aChar;
                                        /* initialise the array */
    for(index = 0; index < alphabetSize; index++)
        frequency[index] = 0;

                            /* read characters and count frequency */
    while((aChar = getchar()) != EOF)
        if(isalpha(aChar))
        {
            index = aChar - (isupper(aChar) ? 'A' : 'a');
            frequency[index]++;
        }
                                        /* display the results */
    printf("Letter  Frequency\n\n");
    for(index = 0; index < alphabetSize; index++)
        printf("  %c    %6d\n", 'a' + index, frequency[index]);
}
```

Note the use of the conditional expression (?:) in determining the correct index value. Having satisfied ourselves that the character is alphabetic, we must find how far it is from the beginning of the alphabet. This conveniently produces values in the range 0..25. When printing the characters, adding this index value onto the character constant 'a' produces the alphabet again. When the program itself is used as input we obtain the following:

```
Letter   Frequency

   a          36
   b           5
   c          21
   d          20
   e          54
   f          16
...
   v           0
   w           1
   x          12
   y          10
   z           0
```

6.1.4 Arrays as Function Arguments

Arrays can be passed as arguments to functions but they appear to be the one exception to the rule, in C, that arguments are always passed by value. In Chapter 7 we discuss the close interrelation between pointers and arrays and explain how they conform to this rule. At the moment, the name of an array appears to represent the whole array but this is not so; the name of an array represents the address of its zeroth element. Until this fuller explanation is possible, we can take the view that array arguments are passed by reference. When the actual argument is an array name, a copy of the whole array is not made; the function is simply told where the array is by being given a copy of its location. This means that when the function accesses an element of the formal argument array, it is the element in the actual argument that is affected.

The above program could be sub-divided into three functions: one to intialise the array, one to compute the frequencies and a third to display the results. The main function would need to declare an array which would be made available to the other three functions. The prototypes for these would be similar to each other:

```
void intialise(int anArray[]);
void buildFequencies(int anArray[]);
void displayFrequencies(int anArray[]);
```

Each function has one argument which is an array of integers. The empty [] indicate that the argument is an array.

The main function declares the array frequency and reserves memory for it. When each of the other functions is called, such as initialise(frequency), this array becomes available to that function. Within initialise(), for example, a reference to the element anArray[index] accesses the array frequency in the calling (main) function. The full program is shown as Program 6.2.

Program 6.2

```
/* to count the frequency of alphabetic letters in the input stream */

#include <stdio.h>
#include <ctype.h>

#define    alphabetSize 26
                                            /* function prototypes */
void initialise(int anArray[]);
void buildFrequencies(int anArray[]);
void displayFrequencies(int anArray[]);

main()
{
   int     frequency[alphabetSize];

   initialise(frequency);
   buildFrequencies(frequency);
   displayFrequencies(frequency);
}

                                            /* initialise an array */
void initialise(int anArray[])
{
   int     index;

   for(index = 0; index < alphabetSize; index++)
      anArray[index] = 0;
}

                             /* read characters and count anArray */
void buildFrequencies(int anArray[])
{
   int     aChar;
   int     index;

   while((aChar = getchar()) != EOF)
      if(isalpha(aChar))
      {
         index = aChar - (isupper(aChar) ? 'A' : 'a');
         anArray[index]++;
      }
}

                                            /* display the results */
void displayFrequencies(int anArray[])
{
   int     index;

   printf("Letter  Frequency\n\n");
   for(index = 0; index < alphabetSize; index++)
      printf("  %c      %6d\n", 'a' + index, anArray[index]);
}
```

In this example, all the arrays are of the same dimension; each function accesses the globally known quantity alphabetSize. Sometimes this is not the case and we want a function to handle whatever array it happens to be given. Under these circumstances it is necessary to pass an extra argument indicating the maximum size of the array.

A function to read a sequence of characters, storing them in a given array could be as:

```c
void getLine(char charArray[], int arraySize)
{
    int     aChar;
    int     index = 0;

    while((aChar = getchar()) != '\n')
        if(index < arraySize - 1) charArray[index++] = aChar;

    charArray[index] = '\0';
}
```

and a small main program to illustrate a use for it:

Program 6.3
_____

```c
#include <stdio.h>

#define    small    20
#define    large    100

void getLine(char charArray[], int arraySize);

main()
{
    char    smallBuffer[small];
    char    largeBuffer[large];

    getLine(smallBuffer,  small);
    getLine(largeBuffer,  large);

    /* do something with these arrays */
}
```
_____

A word of warning: the function getLine() is used here to illustrate a point. There are better functions in the standard library, such as gets() and fgets(), that should be used in practical programs. These are discussed later.

6.1.5   Assignment of Arrays

Comment should be made about the assignment of arrays even though it is negative. Since the name of an array does not represent the whole array but only its location, it is not possible to assign one array to another in one simple statement. Each and every element must be copied individually.

```
#define    maxSize    120

double oldArray[maxSize];
double newArray[maxSize];
int    index;

/* put values into oldArray */

newArray = oldArray;              /* ILLEGAL attempt at assignment */

                                  /* LEGAL - copy every element */
for(index = 0; index < maxSize; index++)
   newArray[index] = oldArray[index];
```

6.1.6   Initialisation

Arrays may be given initial values when they are defined but, in contrast to simple variables, the initial values must be expressed as constants. The form of initialisation is:

```
int    anArray[4] = { 23, 45, 17, 56};
float  another[3] = { 3.5, 7.03, 5.5};
char   vowel[5]   = {'a', 'e', 'i', 'o', 'u'};
```

The dimension need not be specified; the number of initialisers will be used to determine this:

```
int    month[] = {31, 28, 31, 30, 31, 30, 31, 31, 30, 31, 30, 31};
```

6.2 Character Strings

Strings of characters are represented by arrays of type char where the element immediately after the last character of the string is set to the null character, '\0' (i.e. ASCII value 0). The standard library contains a collection of functions for manipulating strings such as copying, concatenation, comparing, finding the length plus functions for input and output. These assume the existence of the terminating null and, where appropriate, insert it. In other situations the responsibility lies with the programmer. Sufficient space must always be reserved in the declaration for the maximum length string plus its trailing '\0'.

The function getLine() tests that index stays below arraySize-1 to ensure that there is at least one element free to hold the terminating '\0'.

Suppose that we wish to strip the leading and trailing blanks from a given character string. We can move an index along the array until we encounter the terminating '\0'; then move back, making sure that we do not go past the beginning; place a new terminating '\0' after the right-most non-blank; finally, we start from the beginning, find the left-most non-blank and then copy character by character so the that the string is placed at the front of the array:

```
void strip(char aString[])
{
   int    right;                    /* index of right end of string */
   int    left;                     /* index of left end of string */

   right = 0;                                   /* find trailing '\0' */
   while(aString[right] != '\0')
      right++;
                                          /* strip trailing blanks */
   left = right -1;
   while(left >= 0  &&  aString[left] == ' ')
      left--;
                                    /* stops on right-most non-blank */
   aString[left+1] = '\0';                     /* add terminating null */


                                     /* find left-most non-blank */
   for(right = 0; aString[right] == ' '; right++)
      ;
                                          /* strip leading blanks */
   for(left = 0; aString[right] != '\0'; left++, right++)
      aString[left] = aString[right];
   aString[left] = '\0';
}
```

Using our function getLine() we can test this in a short main program (Program
6.4).

Program 6.4

```
#include <stdio.h>

#define    bufferSize    80

void getLine(char charArray[], int arraySize);
void strip(char aString[]);

main()
{
   char buffer[bufferSize];

   printf("type a line:");
   getLine(buffer,bufferSize);

   strip(buffer);

   printf("stripped buffer [%s]\n", buffer);
}
```

Sample input(in bold) and output

```
type a line:      a few blanks in between       ⏎
stripped buffer [a few blanks in between]
```

6.2.1   Character String Constants

String constants are represented as a sequence of characters enclosed in double quotes (") :

```
"this is a string constant"
```

The terminating null is automatically provided; hence this string contains 26 characters. Since it is not permissible to assign one array to another, it is not possible to assign a string constant to an array. To do this one usually uses the library function, `strcpy()` which is discussed later. Without this, it would be necessary to copy the string element by element:

```
char    aString[26];
int     index;

aString = "this is a string constant";             /* ILLEGAL */

for(index = 0; index < 26; index)                  /* LEGAL */
    aString[index] = "this is a string constant"[index];

                                        /* use of library function */
strcpy(aString, "this is a string constant");
```

6.2.2   Initialisation

Since character strings are simply arrays of characters the usual method of initialising arrays can be used but you are then responsible for providing the terminating null:

```
char    name[]    = {'f', 'r', 'e', 'd', '\0'};
char    title[3] = {'M', 'r', '\0'};
```

It is however possible to initialise a character array with a string constant. This has the appearance of an assignment but is part of the declaration of the array:

```
char    aString[26] = "this is a string constant";
```

It is important that the dimension of the array is large enough to contain the terminating null. In this case, any dimension greater than 26 would also have been acceptable. In common with all other arrays, it is not necessary to specify the dimension:

```
char    aString[] = "this is a string constant";
```

6.3 Multi-dimensional Arrays

C does not make special provision for multi-dimensioned arrays but simply uses the fact that we can have an array of any type. We merely create an array of arrays. Let us define a type which represents a one-dimensional array, or row, of floats:

```
#define    nCols  6

typedef    float  row[nCols];
```

We can now create another one-dimensional array of rows:

```
#define    nRows  4

row    table[nRows];
```

The variable `table` is made up of 4 rows each of which contains 6   `float` elements. This can be viewed in the more usual rectangular array form as:

```
                          table
```

table[0]	[0][0]	[0][1]	[0][2]	[0][3]	[0][4]	[0][5]
table[1]	[1][0]	[1][1]	[1][2]	[1][3]	[1][4]	[1][5]
table[2]	[2][0]	[2][1]	[2][2]	[2][3]	[2][4]	[2][5]
table[3]	[3][0]	[3][1]	[3][2]	[3][3]	[3][4]	[3][5]

From the declaration of `table`, it follows that `table[1]` is a `row` which is an array of 6 values. Each individual element can thus be accessed by an expression such as `table[1][2]`. The elements of the two-dimensional array are laid out in memory in row order.

[0][0]	[0][1]	[0][2]	[0][3]	[0][4]	[0][5]	[1][0]	[1][1]	[1][2]

This means that if we scan the array in the order in which it is laid out, the rightmost index changes the most quickly.

We would not always choose to use `typedef` in this situation, although it is perfectly legal. We can simply declare a variable to be two-dimensional:

```
float table[nRows][nCols];
```

Note that in both the declaration of the variable and in accessing elements of it, we use multiple pairs of `[]`. It is incorrect to write the form found in other languages:

```
table[row, col]          /* incorrect */
```

Intriguingly, this expression is not illegal! The comma acts as the sequence operator and so the value of the expression within the brackets is simply the value of `col`.

Setting all the elements of this array to zero could be achieved by:

```
int     row;
int     col;

for(col = 0; col < nCols; col++)
    for(row = 0; row < nRows; row++)
        table[row][col] = 0;
```

6.3.1   Function Arguments

When we passed single dimension arrays to functions as their arguments we omitted the size of the dimension but simply used empty [] to show that the argument was, in fact, an array rather than a simple variable. In the case of multi-dimensional arrays we must provide more information. Suppose that we have a function which will transpose a rectangular matrix. It will need two arguments, one for the original matrix and the other for its transpose. The prototype would be:

```
void transpose(float matrix[nRows][nCols],float result[nCols][nRows]);
```

We have observed that a matrix is laid out in consecutive memory locations such that the right-most index changes most quickly. Each individual element can be found if the function knows how many elements are covered by the range of this right-most index. It is thus permissible to omit the first dimension but not the second and subsequent ones:

```
void transpose(float matrix[][nCols],float result[][nRows]);
```

The definition of the function is:

```
void transpose(float matrix[][nCols],float result[][nRows])
{
    int     row;
    int     col;

    for(col = 0; col < nCols; col++)
        for(row = 0; row < nRows; row++)
            result[col][row] = matrix[row][col];
}
```

A piece of program to use this would be like:

```
#define   nRows  20
#define   nCols  30

void transpose(float matrix[][nCols],float result[][nRows]);

main()
{
    float   originalMatrix[nRows][nCols];
    float   transposedMatrix[nCols][nRows];

            /* code to fill original matrix with values goes here*/

    transpose(originalMatrix, transposedMatrix);

            /* code to use the tranposed matrixgoes here */
}
```

Note that the actual argument is just the name of the array. It is the formal argument that needs to be given information about the dimensions.

C does not limit the number of dimensions for an array. The following declaration is perfectly possible:

```
double multiArray[m][n][p][q][r];
```

where m, n, p, q and r are suitably defined constants.

6.3.2   Initialisation

The initialisation of multi-dimensional arrays follows the same pattern as simple arrays.

```
int    table[4][2] ={   { 11, 12},
                        { 21, 22},
                        { 31, 32},
                        { 41, 42}
                    };
```

From this, we can see that the initialiser consists of a comma separated list of 4 items each of which is the initialiser for a 2 element array.

6.4   Structures

Where arrays provide a means of grouping together quantities of the same type, structures allow us to group together quantities of different types. Arrays have elements which are accessible by subscript; structures have components which are accessible by name. Each component can be any simple data type, a pointer, an array or another structure.

   Although not essential, the use of typedef is particularly useful when dealing with structures. Suppose that we wish to represent some characteristics of a person; the following structure would be useful:

```
#define    MaxName    80
                                       /* definition of type person */
typedef    struct {
              char    name[MaxName];
              int     age;
              float   height;
           }
              person;
```

This has defined a new type called person thus enabling us to declare variables of this type:

```
person bert;                           /* declaration of variables */
person mary;
```

These declarations reserve space for two structures of the same type, each consisting of three components:

bert   mary

To access a particular component within one of the variables we use the . (dot) operator:

```
bert.age                          /* of type int */
mary.age                          /* of type int */
bert.height                       /* of type float */
mary.name                         /* of type array of char */
mary.name[3]                      /* of type char */
```

In the last expression there are two operators: . and [ ] . They are of the same precedence and have left to right associativity. This means that the component name is selected from the structure mary and then the element 3 is obtained from that array. We can use each of these quantities in any way appropriate to its type:

```
bert.age = 25;                    /* set his age */
if(mary.age <= bert.age) ...      /* compare ages */
mary.age++;                       /* mary has a birthday */
strcpy(bert.name, "albert Finney"); /* set his name */
bert.name[0] = 'A';               /* change first letter */
```

6.4.1   Arrays of Structures

Now that we have defined a new type, it is a straightforward matter to declare an array of persons:

```
#define    listSize   100

person list[listSize];
```

This gives rise to the following allocation of space:

list

Individual components can be accessed by:

```
list[2].age                    /* of type int */
list[2].height                 /* of type float */
list[2].name                   /* of type array of char */
list[2].name[3]                /* of type char */
```

As we observed above the operators . and [] have the same precedence and left to right associativity; the last expression selects element 2 from the array list, then the component name from that element and, finally, element 3 from name.

6.4.2   Assignment of Structures

C permits the assignment of one structure to another of the same type:

```
person duplicate;
person charles;
                                    /* fill out details of one structure */
strcpy(charles.name, "Charlie Brown");
charles.age = 5;
charles.height = 40;

duplicate = charles;            /* copy one structure to another */
```

The name, age and height of duplicate are now the same as those in charles.

It is important to note that although structures and arrays are both ways of grouping data, C treats them differently. Whereas the name of an array represents its location, the name of a structure represents the complete structure. This means that with respect to assignment: you *cannot assign one array to another in a single expression* but you *can assign one structure to another*. All the contents of the structure on the right hand side of the assignment are copied even though, as in the case of name, a component may itself be an array. It would not however be permissible to assign an array of structures such as list.

Let us illustrate the use of structure assignment together with an array of structures. We wish to build a frequency count of words in a text file, presented to the program as its standard input. We can use the function skipToWord() which we have seen before together with a modification of wordLength(), called getWord(), to obtain successive words from the input stream. We need to record each different word together with its frequency; the following structure, repeatedWord, would be useful:

```
typedef    struct {    char    word[MaxWord];
                       int     frequency;
              }
                       repeatedWord;
```

Program 6.5 sets out the complete program in which, the main function has an array of repeatedWords, list [MaxList]. It uses the function putInList () which is given a new word, the list and the current number of entries in the list. It scans the array to find out if that particular word is already present; if it is the corresponding frequency is incremented; if not, the word is placed in the next empty location at the end of the array, its frequency is set to 1 and the number of entries in the array is incremented. This function returns the number of entries; ideally we would use a variable parameter but until we have looked at pointers, this will do the job. Other functions that are needed are one to sort the list and one to print it.

There are other ways of achieving that same ends. We could have written one of many different sorting algorithms or we could have inserted new words in their correct place so avoiding the need for a sort function.

Program 6.5   (notes and reports the frequency of words)

```c
#include <stdio.h>
#include <string.h>
#include <ctype.h>

typedef enum{ false, true} boolean;

#define MaxWord   80
#define MaxList  200

typedef    struct {    char    word[MaxWord];
                       int     frequency;
                  }
                       repeatedWord;

                                     /* function prototypes */
void       getWord(char word[]);
void       printList(repeatedWord list[], int numberInList);
int        putInList(char word[], repeatedWord list[],
                     int numberInList);
boolean    skipToWord(void);
void       sort(repeatedWord list[], int numberInList);

main()
{
   repeatedWord list[MaxList];
   int          numberInList = 0;

   while(skipToWord())
   {
      char thisWord[MaxWord];

      getWord(thisWord);
      numberInList = putInList(thisWord, list, numberInList);
   }

   sort(list, numberInList);
   printList(list, numberInList);

   printf("\nnumber of words = %d\n", numberInList);
}
```

```
/* ----------------------------------------------------------------
        to skip over white space, stop at a letter or EOF
        if EOF, return false, if at a letter, return true
   ---------------------------------------------------------- */
boolean skipToWord(void)
{
    int aChar;

    do
        aChar = getchar();
    while(aChar != EOF && !isalpha(aChar));

    if(aChar == EOF)
        return false;                   /* indicate end of file */
    else
    {
        ungetc(aChar, stdin);       /* put back extra character */
        return true;                /* indicate that word is found */
    }
}




/* ----------------------------------------------------------------
        to obtain a word from input stream, place it in 'word'
   ---------------------------------------------------------- */
void getWord(char word[])
{
    int ch;
    int k = 0;

    while( isalnum(ch=getchar()))
        word[k++] = ch;                 /* store the character */

    word[k] = '\0';                     /* append terminating null */
    ungetc(ch, stdin);                  /* put back extra character */
}




/* ----------------------------------------------------------------
        to sort repeatedWords in 'list'
   ---------------------------------------------------------- */
void sort(repeatedWord list[], int numberInList)
{
    int i, j;

    for(i = numberInList -1; i>0; i--)
        for(j=0; j<i; j++)
            if(strcmp(list[j].word, list[j+1].word) > 0)
            {
                repeatedWord dummy;
                                     /* exchange adjacent elements */
                dummy      = list[j];
                list[j]    = list[j+1];
                list[j+1]  = dummy;
            }
}
```

```
/* ------------------------------------------------------------------
        to put 'word' in 'list';if it exists,increment its frequency
        if not, add it to the end of 'list'
        return the new number in the list
------------------------------------------------------------------ */
int putInList(char word[], repeatedWord list[], int numberInList)
{
    int     place = 0;

    while( place < numberInList &&
              strcmp(word, list[place].word) != 0)
        place++;                          /* find word in list */

    if(place >= numberInList)        /* is it there? */
    {                                /* no */
        if( numberInList >= MaxList)  /* is there room ? */
            printf("list is full\n"); /* no */
        else                          /* yes */
        {
            numberInList++;               /* one more in list */
            strcpy(list[place].word, word);
            list[place].frequency = 1;
        }
    }
    else    list[place].frequency++; /* repeated word */

    return numberInList;             /* return how many in list */
}


/* ------------------------------------------------------------------
        to display the list of words and frequencies
------------------------------------------------------------------ */
void printList(repeatedWord list[], int numberInList)
{
    int k;

    printf("Identifier    Frequency\n\n");
    for(k = 0; k < numberInList; k++ )
        printf("%-12s%9d\n", list[k].word, list[k].frequency);
}
```

Sample output (using the source file as data input)

Identifier	Frequency
EOF	4
Frequency	1
Identifier	1
MaxList	3
MaxWord	3
a	3
aChar	6
add	1
adjacent	1
and	2

```
        true              3
        typedef           2
        ungetc            2
        void              8
        while             4
        white             1
        word             20
        words             3
        yes               1

        number of words = 121
```

6.4.3   Initialisation

The initialisation of structures adopts the same approach as arrays with the initialising values being placed within braces. In common with arrays these values must be constants:

```
person bert    =  { "Albert", 28, 178};
person list[3] = {   {"Charles", 21, 180},
                     {"Mary", 18, 165},
                     {"James", 35, 182}
               };
employee newOne = { "Frederick", { 23, "September", 1960}};
```

6.4.4   Structures Within Structures

The components of a structure can be of any type and so it follows that a structure can contain another structure. Suppose that we wish to record some limited information about an employee such as their name and date of birth. First, it is useful to have a structure in which to store a date:

```
#define    MaxMonth  10

typedef    struct {
                    int    day;
                    char   month[MaxMonth];
                    int    year;
               }
                    date;
```

Using this, we can define a structure for the employee:

```
#define    MaxName   100

typedef    struct {
                    char   name[MaxName];
                    date   dateOfBirth;    /* struct within struct */
               }
                    employee;
```

The layout of memory for this structure within a structure is thus:

Given the following declarations of variables:

```
employee   fred;
employee   mary;
date       birthday;
```

we can access components such as:

```
fred.name                      /* array of char */
fred.name[2]                   /* char */
fred.dateOfBirth               /* date */
fred.dateOfBirth.day           /* int */
fred.dateOfBirth.month         /* array of char */
fred.dateOfBirth.month[k]      /* char */
```

Since we can assign one structure to another, we are able to write:

```
mary.dateOfBirth = birthday;
```

We are not however able to carry out other operations on structures such as comparison:

```
if(fred.dateOfBirth > mary.dateOfBirth) ...     /* ILLEGAL */
```

6.4.5   Structures and Functions

The ability to assign one structure to another in a single expression means that that function arguments which are structures are readily passed by value in keeping with the general rule. Furthermore it enables functions to return structures.

We have no general way of inputting and outputting structures and must write our own functions to do this. A function to input a date would be useful. Let us model it on the library function getchar() and our own function getint(). A function getdate() reads the input stream and returns the date as a structure:

```
date getdate()
{
    date    aDate;

    aDate.day = getint();
    gets(aDate.month);
    aDate.year    = getint();

    return aDate;
}
```

This could be used in a statement such as:

```
may.dateOfBirth = getdate();
```


6.4.6   Alternative Declarations of Structures

Although we have indicated a preference for the use of typedef with structures, this is not necessary. A type `struct date` could have been defined by putting a tag between the word `struct` and the opening { :

```
#define    MaxMonth  10

struct date    {
                    int     day;
                    char    month[MaxMonth];
                    int     year;
                };
```

The other structure and the variables would be declared as:

```
#define    MaxName    100

struct employee    {
                        char            name[MaxName];
                        struct date     dateOfBirth;
                    };

struct employee  fred;
struct employee  mary;
struct date      birthday;
```

It is also possible to combine the declaration of the structure and variables at the same time:

```
struct employee    {
                        char            name[MaxName];
                        struct date     dateOfBirth;
                    }
                    fred, mary;
```

Additional variables can still be declared as:

```
struct employee  charles, joanna;
```

Finally, it is possible to omit the tag, although this form has very limited use:

```
struct {
          char          name[MaxName];
          struct date   dateOfBirth;
     }
          fred, mary, list[MaxList];
```

This gives us two variables but no means of declaring others of the same type nor of having functions which return this type. It is however the form which, when prefixed by typedef, gives rise to our preferred form.

6.5 Maintaining Some Inventory Records

Program 6.6 conducts a simple dialogue with the user and maintains, in an array of structures of type item, details of some inventory records. The main() function conducts the dialogue, inviting the user to select an option, such as adding a new item, buying or selling some quantity, deleting an item or displaying various details. A switch statement selects another function according to the user's choice.

The array of items is maintained in sorted order with each new entry being put into its correct place, causing other records to be moved along the array.

It is hoped that the comments throughout the program are sufficient to understand what is hapapening.

Program 6.6   (to maintain some inventory records)

```
#include <stdio.h>
#include <stdlib.h>
#include <string.h>

#define    MAXNAME      200
#define    MAXITEMS  10

typedef    struct {
                    char    name[ MAXNAME] ;
                    int     quantity ;
                    long    price ;
               }
                    item ;

typedef char * string ;
typedef enum {false, true} boolean ;
/* function prototypes */
int        addPart(item [], int, item) ;
boolean    changeStock(string, int, item [], int) ;
boolean    deletePart(string, item [], int) ;
void       displayAllParts(item [], int) ;
void       displayPart(string, item [], int) ;
item       getDetails(void) ;
int        indexOf(string, item [], int) ;
void       options(void) ;
```

```c
main()
{
    item    parts[MAXITEMS] ;          /* the  array of stock items */
    int     nParts = 0;                /* number currently in stock */
    char    answer[BUFSIZ] ;           /* temporary buffer for input */

    while( printf("Option ? "), gets( answer) != NULL)
    {
        item    newPart ;              /* temporary new part */
        int     sign = 1 ;             /* +1 for buying,
                                           -1 for selling */
        char    name[ BUFSIZ] ;        /* temporary for input name */

        switch(answer[0])
        {
            case 'n': newPart = getDetails() ;
                      nParts = addPart(parts,nParts,newPart);
                      break ;
            case 'd': printf("which part name ? ") ;
                      gets( name) ;
                      displayPart( name, parts, nParts) ;
                      break ;
            case 'D': displayAllParts( parts, nParts) ;
                      break ;
            case 's': sign = -1 ;
            case 'b': printf("which part name ? ") ;
                      gets( name) ;
                      printf("How much ? ");
                      gets( answer);
                      if(!changeStock( name, sign * atoi( answer),
                                      parts, nParts))
                      printf("Part not Stocked\n");
                      break ;
            case 'r': printf("which part name ? ");
                      gets( name) ;
                      if(deletePart( name, parts, nParts))
                              nParts-- ;
                      else
                              printf("Part not stocked\n");
                      break ;
            case 'q': exit( 0) ;
                      break ;
            default:  printf("Unknown option\n");
            case '?':
            case 'h': options() ;
                      break ;
        }
    }
}
```

```
/* ---------------------------------------------------------------
        to add a newPart to the array of parts
        to return the new number of parts
---------------------------------------------------------------- */
int  addPart(item parts[], int nParts, item newPart)
{
    int    index ;
    int    place = 0 ;

    if( nParts >= MAXITEMS)          /* check size of array */
    {
        fprintf( stderr, " array of parts is full\n") ;
        return nParts ;              /* no change */
    }
                                     /* find correct place */
    while(place < nParts &&
                 strcmp(newPart.name,parts[place].name)>0)
        place++ ;
                                        /* move them up */
    for( index = nParts; index > place ; index-- )          parts[
index] = parts[ index - 1 ] ;

    parts[ place] = newPart ;       /* insert new part */

    return nParts + 1;              /* one extra part stocked */
}




/* ---------------------------------------------------------------
        to increase or decrease the stock of the named part
        to return true if done, false if part not present
---------------------------------------------------------------- */
boolean changeStock(string name, int stockChange,item parts[],
                        int nParts)
{
    int    index = indexOf( name, parts, nParts) ;

    if( index == -1)                          /* not there */
        return false ;
    else
    {
        parts[index].quantity += stockChange;/* increment stock */
        if( parts[index].quantity < 0)       /* no negative stock */
            parts[index].quantity = 0 ;
        return true ;                        /* everything ok */
    }
}
```

```
/* ----------------------------------------------------------------
      to remove the named part
      to return true if done, false if part not present
---------------------------------------------------------------- */
boolean   deletePart(string name, item parts[], int nParts)
{
    int    place = indexOf( name, parts, nParts) ;

    if( place == -1)                              /* not there */
        return false ;
    else
    {
        int    index ;
                              /* close up the list */
        for( index = place ; index < nParts - 1; index ++)
            parts[index] = parts[index + 1] ;

        return true ;                             /* everything ok */
    }
}




/* ----------------------------------------------------------------
      to display the names of all the parts in stock
---------------------------------------------------------------- */
void   displayAllParts(item parts[], int nParts)
{
    int    index ;

    for( index = 0 ; index < nParts; index ++)
        printf("%3d  %s\n", index, parts[index].name);
}




/* ----------------------------------------------------------------
      to display details of the named part
---------------------------------------------------------------- */
void   displayPart(string name, item parts[], int nParts)
{
    int    index ;

    if((index = indexOf( name, parts, nParts)) == -1)
        printf("Part not held\n");
    else
        printf("\t\t\t%-15s%s\n\t\t\t%-15s%d\n\t\t\t%-15s%d\n",
            "Part name", parts[index].name,
            "Stock in hand", parts[index].quantity,
            "Selling price", parts[index].price ) ;
    return;
}
```

```
/* ----------------------------------------------------------------
       to obtain details for a new part for stdin
   --------------------------------------------------------------- */
item    getDetails(void)
{
   item    newOne ;                      /* temporary new part */
   char    line[ BUFSIZ] ;               /* temporary input buffer */

   printf("Name ? ");
   gets( newOne.name) ;
   printf("Opening stock ? ") ;
   newOne.quantity = atoi( gets( line)) ;
   printf("Selling price ? ") ;
   newOne.price = atoi( gets(line)) ;

   return newOne ;
}



/* ----------------------------------------------------------------
   to return the numerical index of the named part in the list
   to return -1 if not present
   --------------------------------------------------------------- */
int     indexOf(string name, item parts[], int nParts)
{
   int     index = 0 ;

   while( index < nParts && strcmp( parts[ index].name, name) != 0)
      index++ ;

   if( index >= nParts)                  /* not there */
      return -1 ;
   else
      return index;                      /* found it */
}
/* ----------------------------------------------------------------
   to display list of options
   --------------------------------------------------------------- */
void    options(void)
{
   printf("\nn\tNew part\n");
   printf("d\tDisplay a part\n");
   printf("D\tDisplay all part names\n");
   printf("s\tSell some material\n");
   printf("b\tBuy some material\n");
   printf("r\tRemove an item from stock\n");
   printf("q\tQuit\n");
   printf("? h\tThis list\n\n");
}
```

Sample input(in bold) and output
_____

```
Option ? ?

n   New part
d   Display a part
D   Display all part names
s   Sell some material
b   Buy some material
r   Remove an item from stock
q   Quit
? h    This list

Option ? n
Name ? widgets
Opening stock ? 250
Selling price ? 23.50
Option ? n
Name ? gadget grease
Opening stock ? 120
Selling price ? 15.60
Option ? D
  0   gadget grease
  1   widgets
Option ? d
which part name ? widgets
          Part name      widgets
          Stock in hand  250
          Selling price  23
Option ? d
which part name ? grommets
Part not held
Option ? s
which part name ? widgets
How much ? 85
Option ? d
which part name ? widgets
          Part name      widgets
          Stock in hand  165
          Selling price  23
Option ? q
```
_____

6.6 Unions

Unions are similar to structures in both the way that they are declared and the way in which their components are accessed. They only differ, apart from the name `union` instead of `struct`, in that their components overlap in memory instead of each component being allocated its own territory.

Suppose that we wish to use an array of geometric shapes. Although we may wish to handle points, lines and circles, each element of the array would represent only one such shape. If we had a type `geometricShape` we could declare:

```
geometricShape   listOfShapes[MaxList];
```

If we had some types for individuals geometric shapes:

```
typedef struct    {   float  x,y; }     point;

typedef struct    {   float  a, b, c; } line;

typedef struct    {   point  centre;
                      float  radius; } circle;
```

We could then define our required general type `geometricShape`:

```
typedef enum {pointType, lineType, circleType} shapeType;

typedef struct    {   shapeType shape;
                      union {   point  thePoint;
                                line   theLine;
                                circle theCircle;
                            }
                                actualShape;
                  }
                      geometricShape;
```

It is common practice to include an enumerative type, `shapeType`, so that when accessing the structure, `actualShape`, we know which of the components of the union is relevant. The `switch` statement:use with unions is particularly useful in this context. A general function to display a shape would be like:

```
void displayShape (geometricShape aShape)
{
    switch (aShape.shape)
    {
        case pointType:   displayPoint (aShape.actualShape.thePoint);
                          break;
        case lineType:    displayLine (aShape.actualShape.theLine);
                          break;
        case circleType:  displayCircle (aShape.actualShape.theCircle);
                          break;
        default:          printf("Error: incorrect shape specified\n");
                          break;
    }
}
```

which, in turn, enables us to scan the array of shapes displaying each one:

```
void displayShape (geometricShape aShape);
void displayPoint (point aPoint);
void displayLine  (point aLine);
void displayCircle(point aCircle);

main()
{
    geometricShape   listOfShapes[MaxList];
    int              k;

    /* fill the array of shapes with something useful */

    for(k = 0; k < MaxList; k++)
        displayShape(listOfShapes[k]);
}
```

7

Pointers

Many people, approaching C for the first time, are apprehensive about the concept of pointers, having learnt from others that they can present difficulties. There is no need to be cautious. Pointers form a valuable and important part of the language, helping to give it its power. Having said this, their incorrect use can give rise to some elusive errors.

When we declare a variable, the compiler decides which piece of memory is to be allocated for it. Each and every part of memory has its own unique address and it is possible, in C, to find where any variable is stored. That is, the programer can find the address of any variable. A *pointer* is simply a special type of variable which is capable of storing the addresses of other variables. When it does do so, it is said, not surprisingly, to point to that second variable.

There are three main uses for pointers:

a) variable arguments to functions, overcoming the *call by value* restriction

b) dynamic data structures; e.g. to create and handle linked lists and trees

c) accessing the elements of arrays; as an alternative to subscripting.

The first two can only be achieved by the use of pointers and although it is possible to access arrays by subscripts, it is commonplace for C programmers to use pointers. Even if for no other reason, it is important to understand their use in this context so that you can read other people's programs.

7.1 Pointer Notation

When we declare a variable, say `anInteger`, the compiler allocates a piece of memory and notes its address.

```
int     anInteger;
```

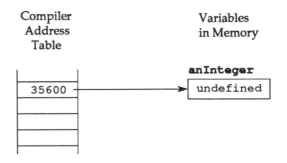

We can find out this address by using the prefix operator & (address of operator). In this case, &anInteger has the value 35600. To satisfy our curiosity we can print this by using:

```
printf("The address of the variable anInteger is \d\n", &anInteger);
```

which produces:

```
The address of the variable anInteger is 35600
```

To be able to use addresses in a meaningful way we need to be able to store them in other variables. The only real problem is to decide what is the type of such a variable. A variable which is capable of storing the addresses of int variables is declared to be of type int * and is called a *pointer to int*. Let us create a variable called ptrInteger:

```
int *  ptrInteger;
```

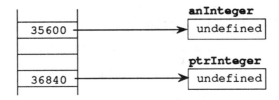

In common with all other variables, a pointer has no meaningful value until one has been assigned to it. The declaration merely states what the capability of a variable is. The variable anInteger is <u>capable of holding an integer</u> value even though it does not have one at the moment. In a similar way, the pointer ptrInteger is <u>capable of holding the address of an integer</u> even though it does not have one at the moment.

We can remedy this by giving it the value of the address of `anInteger`:

```
ptrInteger = &anInteger;
```

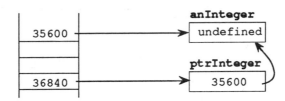

Only now can we say that the variable `ptrInteger` points to the variable `anInteger`. Note that `ptrInteger`, in turn, has an address but let us not concern ourselves with using that at the moment.

The integer variable `anInteger` can now be accessed directly by means of its name or indirectly by means of the variable `ptrInteger` which points to it. Clearly, direct access is the more natural but, for the purposes mentioned above, we will need to know how to use indirect access. The indirection operator `*`, a prefix operator, is needed. The expression `*ptrInteger` yields contents of the location to which `ptrInteger` points which is different from the expression `ptrInteger` which yields the address of the location to which it points. Let us assign a value to `anInteger` directly:

```
anInteger = 713;
```

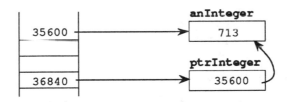

The following is now valid:

```
printf("The value at location \d is \d\n", ptrInteger, *ptrInteger);
```

which produces:

```
The value at location 35600 is 713
```

We can use the expression `*ptrInteger` in any way that we would use an integer:

```
if( *ptrInteger > 250) ...          /* in comparison */
result = 25 + *ptrInteger;          /* in arithmetic */
*ptrInteger = 862;                  /* in assignment */
```

after this last assignment the variable, `anInteger`, contains the value 862:

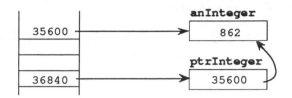

7.1.1 Pointer Types

Every type of data in the language can have a pointer type associated with it. It is however most important to remember that *each pointer type is different*. Consider the following declarations:

```
int       count, index;
float     temperature;
char      letter;

int *     ptrInt;
float *   ptrFloat;
char *    toChar;
```

Each of the three pointer types is different so that the following assignments are legal:

```
ptrInt   = &count;
prtInt   = &index;
ptrFloat = &temperature;
toChar   = &letter;
```

The following are however illegal:

```
ptrFloat = &count;  /* cannot assign address of int to float *   */
prtInt   = &letter; /* cannot assign address of char to int *    */
```

We have placed the * in the declaration near to the base type to emphasise that the types are `int *`, `float *` and `char *`. However it is commonplace to adjoin it to the variable:

```
int    *ptrInt, count, *ptrA;
float  temperature, *ptrFloat;
char   *toChar, letter, buffer[Max];
char   *ptrArray[Max];
```

The first declares `prtInt` and `prtA` as type `int *` and count as type `int`. The type is seen to be split into two parts. The third declaration reminds us that we are already familiar with this idea with respect to arrays. The variable `buffer` is an array of `char` whereas `letter` is a `char` and `toChar` is of type `char *`. The final declaration sets out `ptrArray` as an array of `char *`; i.e. an array of pointers to characters.

There is a danger of confusing the use of * in the declaration and its use as the prefix indirection operator in expressions. Once the variable ptrA has been assigned a legitimate value and points to an integer, the expression *ptrA will yield an integer. On the other hand, the declaration:

```
int     *ptrA;
```

does not give an integer; it merely defines a variable ptrA, of type int *, which is capable of pointing to an integer. It does not yet point to one and so the subsequent use of the expression *ptrA would be invalid until ptrA were assigned an address of an integer.

7.1.2   Simple Uses of Pointers

A pointer does not have to remain tied to one variable throughout its whole existence. Although it can only point to one variable at any one time, it may point to different variables at different times. On the other hand it is perfectly feasible for many pointers to point to a single variable at the same time. In fact, this is commonplace in programs.

```
int     *ptrA, *ptrB;
int     anInteger, another;

anInteger = 49;
ptrA      = &anInteger;
ptrB      = another;
```

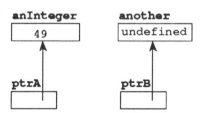

ptrA points to anInteger which has the value 49 and ptrB points to another which itself is undefined. After the following:

```
*ptrB = *ptrA;              /* assignment of ints */
ptrA  = ptrB;               /* assignment of pointers to int */
```

the object to which ptrB points, namely another, has taken the value of the object to which ptrA points, namely, anInteger; and then ptrA has taken the value of ptrB, meaning that these two pointers now point to the same object:

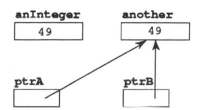

At some further stage in the computation we could find out whether the two integers to which the pointers point, contain the same value and we could also find out whether the two pointers point to the same object:

```
if(ptrA == ptrB)                            /* pointer comparison */
    printf("they point to the same object ");
else
{
    printf("they point to different objects ");
    if(*ptrA == *ptrB)                      /* integer comparison */
        printf("but the objects have the same value\n");
    else
        printf("and the objects have different values\n");
}
```

Meaningful comparisons for pointers are thus == (do they point to the same object?) and != (do they point to different objects?). When we discuss the role of pointers in accessing array elements the relational operators >, >=, < and <= will have some purpose.

7.2 Constant Pointer NULL

There are occasions when we wish a pointer to have a legally defined value but we do not want it to point to a particular object. The constant NULL, defined in the header file stddef.h represents the value 0 which is guaranteed to be different from all legal pointer values. We may thus assign the value NULL to a pointer and we may compare a pointer with this value:

```
ptrB = NULL;                                /* now points to nothing */

...

if(ptrA == NULL)                            /* pointer comparison */
    printf("it does not point to anything");
else
    printf("it points to an object");

if(ptrB != NULL)
    printf("it points to an object");
else
    printf("it does not point to anything");
```

7.3 Pointers to Structures

The use of pointers to structures introduces some new notation. Suppose that we
have a structure type, `Person`, representing the details of a person together with
some variables:

```
typedef    struct {    char    name[MaxName];
                       int     age;
                       float   height;
                   }
                       Person;

Person employee;
Person *ptrPerson = &employee;
```

From what we have discussed above, the object to which `ptrPerson` points is
obtained by `*ptrPerson`. It would thus seem reasonable to access the
components of this structure by the `.` (dot) operator, e.g. `*ptrPerson.age`.
Unfortunately, when we consult the table of precedence and associativity, we find
that the dot (`.`) operator has higher precedence than the indirection (`*`) operator
thus causing this expression to fail. We need to use parentheses to change the order:

```
(*ptrPerson).name                    /* array of char */
(*ptrPerson).name[k]                 /* char */
(*ptrPerson).age                     /* int */
(*ptrPerson).height                  /* float */
```

Although these are perfectly legal expressions, accessing a structure by means of a
pointer is a sufficiently common activity for an alternative notation to be provided.
The components can be accessed directly from the pointer with the aid of the `->`
operator.

```
ptrPerson->name                      /* array of char */
ptrPerson->name[k]                   /* char */
ptrPerson->age                       /* int */
ptrPerson->height                    /* float */
```

In the second expression we have two operators, `->` and `[]`. These have the same
precedence and associate from left to right. Without additional parentheses we
fortunately achieve the meaning that we want.

Consider now, two different situations, one in which a structure contains another structure and the other in which a structure contains a pointer to another structure:

```
typedef    struct {   int     day;
                      char    month[MaxMonth];
                      int     year;
                  }
                      Date;

typedef    struct {   char    name[MaxName];
                      Date    dateOfBirth;              /* a structure */
                  }
                      PersonWithDate;

typedef    struct {   char    name[MaxName];
                                              /* pointer to structure */
                      Date    *refDateOfBirth;
                  }
                      PersonWithRefDate;

PersonWithDate        employee;
PersonWithDate        *ptrEmployee = &employee;
PersonWithRefDate     manager;
PersonWithRefDate     *ptrManager  = &manager;
Date                  birth;

                              /* give the structures some values */
strcpy(employee.name, "Alexander Bumblehurst");
employee.dateOfBirth.day = 13;
strcpy(employee.dateOfBirth.month, "March");
employee.dateOfBirth.year = 1966;


                                  /* set up variable manager */
strcpy(manager.name, "James Superior");
manager.refDateOfBirth = &birth;
                                  /* set his date of birth */
manager.refDateOfBirth->day = 24;
strcpy(manager.refDateOfBirth->month, "June");
manager.refDateOfBirth->year = 1944;
```

the layout of these variables is now:

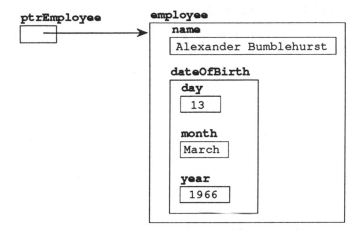

some legal expressions are:

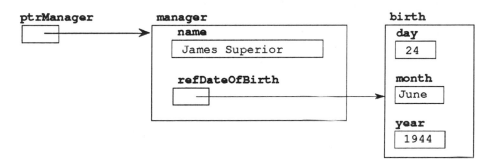

```
                                    /* TYPE: */
ptrEmployee->dateOfBirth            /* Date */
ptrEmployee->dateOfBirth.month      /* array of char */
ptrEmployee->dateOfBirth.month[2]   /* char */

ptrManager->name                    /* array of char */
ptrManager->refDateOfBirth          /* pointer to Date */
ptrManager->refDateOfBirth->month   /* array of char */
ptrManager->refDateOfBirth->month[3] /* char */

*(ptrManager->refDateOfBirth)       /* Date */
```

In summary, we have two ways of accessing the components of a structure:

• *structureVariable.component*

• *pointerToStructure->component*

7.4 Variable Arguments to Functions

We have noted that one important use of pointers is to enable us to create variable arguments to functions. By *a variable argument* we mean that the function being called can change the actual argument which has apparently been passed to it. However, we have also noted that all arguments are passed by value which means that the function being called is given a copy of the actual argument. The formal argument of the function is a local variable which is initialised to the value of the actual argument. It is able to change its formal argument, namely the copy, but such a change has no effect on the actual argument.

For a called function to be able the alter a variable local to the calling function, it must know where that variable is. If we were to give the called function a copy of the address of the variable in question, it would be able to alter the variable by means of indirection. The formal argument would need to be of pointer type and the actual argument would need to be the address of the variable in question.

Let us look at an example in which a function, `callingFunction()`, has two local integer variables: `first` and `second`. This function calls another function, `func()`, such that the first argument is a call by value and the second is a call by reference. The prototype for this function will be:

```
void func(int arg1, int * arg2);
```

This can then be called by: `func(first, &second);`

Program extract

```
void func(int arg1, int * arg2);

void callingFunction()
{
    int     first  = 71;
    int     second = 94;

    printf("before the call: first = %d second = %d", first, second);
    func(first, &second);       /* note the address of operator (&) */
    printf("after the call:  first = %d second = %d", first, second);
}

void func(int arg1, int * arg2)
{
    arg1  =   82;
    *arg2 = 105;                          /* note the indirection by *    */
}
```

Sample output

```
before the call: first = 71 second =   94
after the call:  first = 71 second = 105
```

Let us consider this diagrammatically.

Stage 1:   Before the function, `func()`, is called we have two local variables, `first` and `second`, in `callingFunction()` and two arguments, `arg1` and `arg2`, in `func()`:

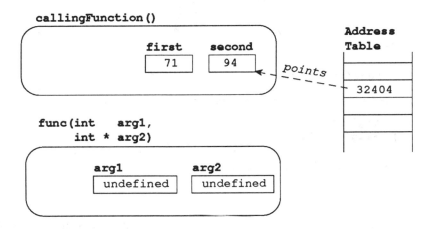

Stage 2:   Immediately after the function has been called, we note that the *value of* `first` has been copied into `arg1` and the *address of* `second` into `arg2`:

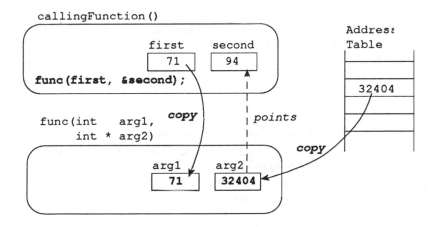

Stage 3: Assigning a new value to `arg1` does not affect the actual argument, `first`; assigning a new value to the variable *to which* `arg2` *points* does affect the variable `second`:

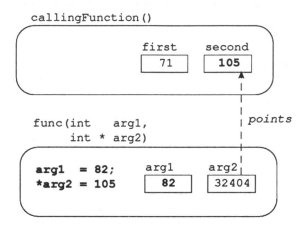

In summary, C does not support directly the concept of variable arguments or *call by reference*. All actual arguments are passed by value. In our example, the variable `first` uses a direct call by value which results in a change of `arg1` being separate from the value of `first`. To enable the variable `second` to be changed by the function, a number of steps need to be taken:

• the *address of* second needs to be passed

• the formal argument, `arg2`, needs to be a *pointer*

• *indirection* from this argument allows us to alter the variable `second`.

It is most important to note that this approach places a responsibility on the user as well as on the designer of the function. The user needs to remember to pass an address, whilst the designer of the function needs to use indirection properly.

7.4.1 The Actual Argument Must Point To Something

This last point is of great importance: the user has a responsibility to handle the actual argument correctly. Suppose we have available a function `getDate()` which will prompt the user of the application for details of a date and will return these via its argument. A possible prototype would be:

```
void getDate(Date *aDate);
```

In the calling function, we may decide that an actual argument of the same type as the formal argument should be provided by:

```
void callingFunction()
{
    Date    *birthDate;

    getDate(birthDate);                  /* ERROR */
    . . .
}
```

Although the actual and formal arguments are of the same type, the actual argument `birthDate` does not point to anything and so when the function `getDate()` attempts to indirect from its formal argument `aDate`, a problem occurs. It is absolutely essential that a quantity of type `Date` is created in the calling function.

```
void callingFunction()
{
    Date    birthDate;                   /* reserve space for a Date */
    Date    *ptrDate;

    getDate(&birthDate);                       /* pass the address */

/* an alternative approach: */

    ptrDate = &birthDate;        /* point to something worthwhile */

    getDate(ptrDate);                        /* pass the pointer */

}
```

Either approach is correct. Whichever way we choose to pass the address to the function `getDate()`, a place to receive the date has been created. It should be noted that instead of the assignment of the address to the pointer variable it would have been acceptable to initialise the pointer variable at the time of definition:

```
Date *ptrDate = & birthDate;
```

7.5 The Type void *

Certain library functions need to make use of a generic pointer. The memory allocation function `malloc()` and its relatives, the low level input/output functions `fread()` and `fwrite()`, the searching function `bsearch()` and the sorting function `qsort()` all have arguments which point to quantities. However the writers of these functions could not possibly have known what type of quantities you or I would want to search or sort and so they could only make use a generic pointer.

For this purpose the type `void *` has been introduced. Prior to the ANSI Standard, the type `char *` was used.

There are some points to note here:

•   any pointer type can be assigned to a variable of type `void *`

•   it is not possible to indirect from a variable or expression of type `void *`; casting to another pointer is needed before this can be done

Having said this, you are unlikely to need to create your own functions which use these generic pointers; at least not in your early stages of programming in C. You are however likely to need to use some of the library functions. We will discuss the memory allocation function `malloc()` in the next chapter and take that opportunity to illustrate the use of `void *`.

7.6 Accessing Arrays by Pointers

Arrays and pointers have a very close relationship in C. Although elements of arrays can always be accessed by subscripts and scanned by means of an integer index, these operations are frequently more efficient when pointers are used. When we declare an array of elements (of any type), space is reserved:

```
#define    ArraySize 150

anyType    anArray[ArraySize]; /* allocate space for 150 elements */
```

The typical way in which we would scan this array, accessing its elements would be:

```
#define    ArraySize 150
anyType    anArray[ArraySize]; /* allocate space for 150 elements */
int        index;

for(index = 0; index < ArraySize; index++)
    process(anArray[index]);
```

As an alternative we could use a pointer, `toArray`:

```
#define    ArraySize 150
anyType    anArray[ArraySize]; /* allocate space for 150 elements */
anyType    *toArray;

for(toArray = anArray; toArray < anArray + ArraySize; toArray++)
    process(*toArray);
```

A number of points needed to be noted:

- **the name of an array represents the address of its zeroth element:**
  `toArray = anArray`

  this is equivalent to `toArray = &anArray[0]`

- when incrementing a pointer which is pointing to an element of an array, the pointer moves on to the next element, regardless of the type of that element:
  `toArray++`

- arithmetic can be performed with addresses:
  `anArray + ArraySize`

- comparisons can be made between addresses:
  `toArray < anArray + ArraySize`

Assuming that we have made the assigment `toArray = anArray`, the following expressions are equivalent:

Addresses:

```
anArray                 toArray                &anArray[0]
anArray + 1             toArray + 1            &anArray[1]
anArray + k             toArray + k            &anArray[k]
```

Elements at the addresses:

```
*anArray                *toArray               anArray[0]
* (anArray + 1)         * (toArray + 1)        anArray[1]
* (anArray + k)         * (toArray + k)        anArray[k]
```

Parentheses are needed in these expressions since, without them, the indirection operator * would take effect before the addition:

```
*anArray + k            *toArray + k           anArray[0] + k
```

We can show these diagrammatically:

```
toArray = anArray;
```

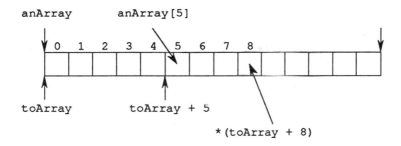

after the pointer has been incremented we will have:

```
toArray++;
```

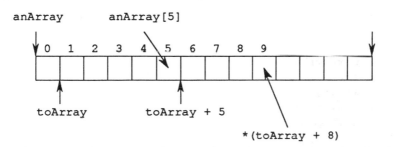

Let us consider a program written in both subscript (Program 7.1) and pointer form (Program 7.2). This will scan an array of characters, `message`, searching for a given sub-string, `word`. The real work is done by a library function `strncmp()` which compares its first and second arguments, comparing no more characters than indicated by its third argument. It returns a value of zero it the two strings match. We need to scan the larger string, message, testing whether the second string, word, matches.

Program 7.1   (using subscripts)

```
/* to find a substring in a longer string - using subscripts */

#include <stdio.h>
#include <stdlib.h>
#include <string.h>

#define    MaxWord        256

main()
{
    char message[] = "will it work with this string";
    char            word[MaxWord];

    printf("The test string is: '%s'\n", message);

    while(printf("Substring: "),gets(word) != NULL)
    {
        int here = 0;

        while(message[here] != '\0' &&
              strncmp(&message[here], word, strlen(word)) != 0)
            here++;

        if(message[here] == '\0')
            printf("not found\n");
        else
            printf("found at position %d\n", here);
    }

    exit(EXIT_SUCCESS);
}
```

Sample input (in bold) and output

```
The test string is: 'will it work with this string'
Substring: will↵
found at position 0
Substring: work with↵
found at position 8
Substring: string↵
found at position 23
Substring: stringy↵
not found
```

Each of the first two arguments to strncmp() needs the address of the first character of a string. The use of the 'address of' operator is therefore needed. When we rewrite this program to use pointers instead of subscripts, the variable, here, becomes a char * instead of an int. Since this pointer is incremented so that it points, in turn, to each character in message, we can use it directly in the inner while loop. It should be noted that, in each version of the program, this inner while loop could have been written as a for loop.

Program 7.2   (using pointers)

```
/* to find a substring in a longer string - using pointers */

#include <stdio.h>
#include <stdlib.h>
#include <string.h>

#define    MaxWord        256

main()
{
    char message[] = "will it work with this string";
    char             word[MaxWord];

    printf("The test string is: '%s'\n", message);

    while(printf("Substring: "),gets(word) != NULL)
    {
        char   *here = message;

        while(*here != '\0' &&
              strncmp(here, word, strlen(word)) != 0)
            here++;

        if(*here == '\0')
            printf("not found\n");
        else
            printf("found at position %d\n", here - message);
    }

    exit(EXIT_SUCCESS);
}
```

It is most important to remember that we are using pointers only to access the elements of the array. We still need to declare the arrays, message and word, in the usual way.

7.6.1   Interchangability of Pointers and Array Names

Let us now look more closely at the interrelationship between pointers and arrays. Consider the following set of declarations:

```
#define    ArraySize 14

int    array1[ArraySize];
int    array2[ArraySize];
int    *ptr1 = array1;
int    *pyr2 = array2;
```

A diagram displaying this, together with possible compiler table addresses would be:

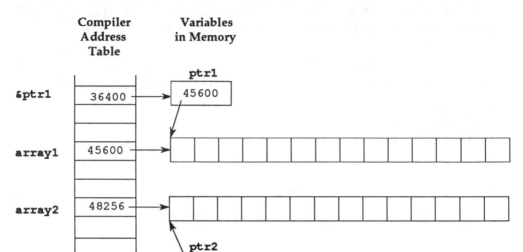

We rarely need to know the actual values of the addresses but it helps to illustrate what is happening here.

In certain ways the array name and the pointer which is associated with it are interchangeable. Each of the following is permissible:

```
int     index;

for(index = 0; index < ArraySize; index++);
    array1[index] = index;

for(index = 0; index < ArraySize; index++);
    ptr1[index] = index;

for(index = 0; index < ArraySize; index++);
    *(array1 + index) = index;

for(index = 0; index < ArraySize; index++);
    *(ptr1 + index) = index;
```

The pointer can appear to be an array name and the array name can appear to be a pointer. A most important difference, however, is that the pointer is a variable whose value, in this case, happens to be the address of the first element of the array; whereas the array name represents an entry in the compiler address table and is thus a constant. It is for this reason that we are unable to assign one array to another in one simple statement such as:

```
array1 = array2;                              /*ILLEGAL */
```

This takes the address of the zeroth element of array2, namely 48256, and attempts to replace the entry 45600 in the compiler table. This is clearly not possible because if it were, the programmer could decide during the execution of the program where variables should be placed in memory; this is a job for the compiler.

A similar assignment for pointers is possible but it would still not assign complete arrays:

```
ptr1 = ptr2;
```

After this our diagram would appear as:

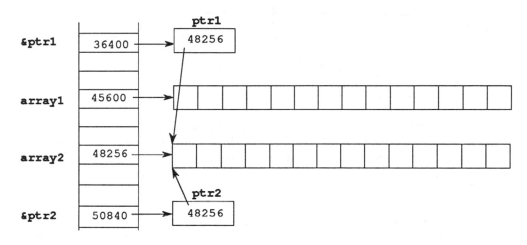

Both pointers now point to array2 and ptr1 has become disassociated from array1.

As we can see from this, pointers are variables whose values can be changed. Other possibilities include:

```
ptr1 += 3;
ptr2++;
```

At this stage, the diagram becomes:

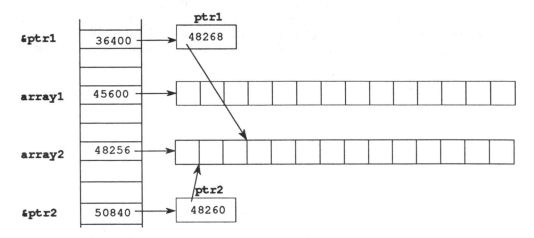

A most important point to note here is that all arithmetic with pointers takes note of the size of the objects to which they are pointing. Since we have used ints as the elements of the arrays, the actual values of the pointers have changed by multiples of 4 (on my computer). It is however better to think only in terms of the objects to which they point than the addresses stored in the pointers. Incrementation by ++ moves the pointer on by one element.

It is for this reason that every pointer type is regarded as different. No matter what type of element is used in an array, the pointer moves onto the very next element when it is incremented by one.

Possible arithmetic operations are:

Expression			Result
pointer	+	integer	pointer
integer	+	pointer	pointer
pointer	−	integer	pointer
pointer	−	pointer	integer

The last expression determines the distance, in number of elements, between two pointers. For this to make any sense, the two pointers must be pointing to elements of the same array. If they are not, the result is meaningless. When two pointers are pointing to elements in the same array, it is possible to compare their values. We are assured that the addresses of consecutive elements in an array will have ascending addresses.

Given a situation such as:

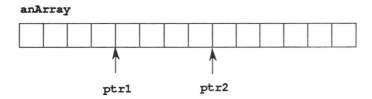

we can make use any of the six relational operators: <, <=, >, >=, ==, !=.   Some illustrative code would be:

```
if(ptr1 < ptr2)          printf("ptr1 is to the left of ptr2\n");
else if(ptr1 == ptr2)    printf("they point to the same element\n"):
else                     printf("ptr1 is to the right of ptr2\n");

if(ptr1 >= ptr2)         printf("ptr2 is to the left of ptr1\n");

if(ptr1 != ptr2)         printf("they point to different elements\n");
```

Returning to subscript notation, for the moment, and referring the to diagram where ptr1 points to the array2[3], the following are equivalent:

```
array2[0]        ptr1[-3]        *(ptr - 3)
array2[1]        ptr1[-2]        *(ptr - 2)
array2[2]        ptr1[-1]        *(ptr - 1)
array2[3]        ptr1[0]         *ptr
array2[4]        ptr1[1]         *(ptr + 1)
...
```

A final, intriguing aspect arises from the fact that subscript notation is implicitly converted to pointers: array[index] becomes *(array + index); but the order of addition cannot matter, so this is the same as *(index + array) which, in turn, is the equivalent of index[array]!! It is possible, although admittedly unusual and not recommended, to write:

```
for(index = 0; index < ArraySize; index++)
    index[array] = index;
```

7.6.2   Incrementation and Access

When manipulating arrays it is commonplace to combine the incrementation of the pointer with access to the element to which it is pointing, such as *ptr++. Since the ++ operator can be used in either its pre-fix or post-fix form and we can either increment the pointer itself or the element to which it is pointing, many possibilities arise. The table of precedence of operators reminds us that these two operators have the same level of precedence but that they associate from right to left.

Consider the situation in which we have a pointer ptr pointing to an element of an array and another variable result. Four different expressions each of whose values can be assigned to result can be considered in turn. Each expression will be considered independently and will assume the following situation immediately prior to its execution:

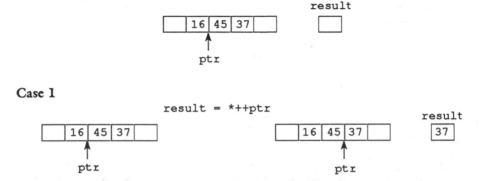

Case 1

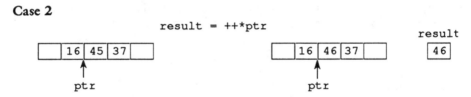

The associativity of the operators means that ++ is applied to ptr *before* indirection takes place; thus ptr moves on one element and result is given the value to which ptr is now pointing.

Case 2

result = ++*ptr

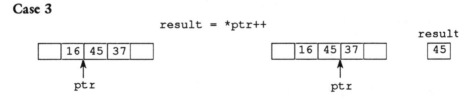

In this case, the indirection from ptr comes first and it is this value which is incremented. Because we have a pre-fix operator, the incrementation takes place before the assignment.

Case 3

result = *ptr++

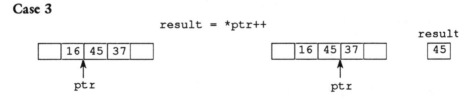

This is similar to case 1 except that the incrementation is now post-fix. The associativity rule means that incrementation is *applied to ptr before the indirection* but the post-fix nature of the incrementation means that its *effect is delayed until after the assignment*. The pointer is moved on but the value given to result is that to which ptr originally pointed.

Case 4

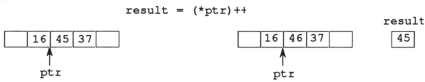

Parentheses are now needed to change the order in which the incrementation and indirection are performed. This change means that the element to which ptr points is now incremented but, because the incrementation is post-fix, this incrementation is performed *after* the assignment .

We can also consider using these expressions on the left hand side of the assignment operator. Two of them, namely (*ptr)++ and ++*ptr, are illegal because each attempts to increment a non-pointer thus producing an illegal L-value. The others which increment pointers are legal. We will again use the same starting conditions for each of these expressions.

Case 5

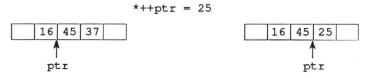

The effects of the associativity rule and the pre-fix nature of the incrementation are the same as in case 1: ptr is moved on and then the element to which it points is assigned a value.

Case 6

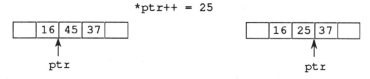

The only difference here is that the incrementation is now post-fix and so its effect on the pointer is delayed until after the assignment. The element to which it originally points is altered by the assignment.

7.7 Arrays as Function Arguments

In Section 6.1.4 we stated, rather boldly, that *array arguments are passed by reference*. This is not, in fact, true, they only *appear* to be passed by reference. Actual arguments are *always passed by value*. By this we mean that a copy of the actual argument is made to intialise the formal argument which, itself, has the role of a local variable to the function.

We are now able to explain why arrays appear to be handled differently. A typical situation would be:

```
#define    MaxSize    120

void    handleArray(int  anArray[]);                    /* prototype */

void    callingFunction()
{
    int    localArray[MaxSize];

    ...
    handleArray(localArray);
    ...
}

void    handleArray(int  anArray[])            /* function definition */
{
    int    index;

    for(index = 0; index < MaxSize; index++)
        process(anArray[index]);
}
```

We now know that the name of an array represents the address of its zeroth element. When we call a function such as handleArray(localArray), we are in fact copying this address to the formal argument. The type that can store an address is a pointer and so the correct type of the formal argument, anArray, would seem to be int *. The function prototype is, strictly speaking:

```
void    handleArray(int  *anArray);                    /* prototype */
```

The formal argument is really a pointer and any subscripting inside the function such as anArray[index] is implicitly converted to the equivalent form of *(anArray + index). In the declaration of the arguments, the style using [] is simply an alternative to the pointer notation; this alternate notation is only for use in this context.

Consider, as an example, a function which accepts an array of characters and determines whether it is palindromic, i.e. it is the same when read backwards. We examine the outside pair of characters and if they are equal work steadily towards the centre, repeating the comparison. This is set out in Program 7.3.

The variables anArray, left and right are all local with left and the formal argument, anArray, both initialised to the address of the array aSentence in main(). As the pointers left and right are incremented and decremented respectively, they point to elements in the array aSentence. Examining these elements is performed by indirection.

Program 7.3

```c
/* to determine whether a given character string is palindromic

   using pointers to arrays
*/

#include <stdio.h>
#include <stdlib.h>

#define    MaxSentence       120

typedef enum {false, true} boolean;

boolean isPalindromic(char *anArray);

main()
{
    char    aSentence[MaxSentence];

    while(printf("Type a line: "), gets(aSentence) != NULL)
        if(isPalindromic(aSentence))
            printf("this is palindromic\n");
        else
            printf("this is not palindromic\n");

    exit(EXIT_SUCCESS);
}

boolean isPalindromic(char *anArray)
{
    char    *left = anArray;          /* initialise the left pointer */
    char    *right;

                                      /* find right hand end */
    for(right = anArray; *right != '\0'; right++)
        ;

    right--;                          /* set the right pointer */
    while(left <= right && *left == *right)
    {
        left++;                       /* increment the pointer */
        right--;
    }

    if(left >= right)return true;
    else             return false;
}
```

7.7.1   A Notational Style

When we have available to us, possibly in a commercial library, a function which has a pointer as one of its arguments, how do we know whether this refers to an array or to a single quantity? The simple answer is that we do not!

Suppose that we have a function which places a name into a structure representing a person:

```
void    insertName(Person *, char *);
```

Without a clear verbal description it is not obvious that the first argument is intended to be a pointer to a single structure but that the second is to be a pointer to the beginning of a character array. A suitable choice of variable names can be a help:

```
void    insertName(Person *aPerson, char *name);
```

Inside the function, the code could be something like the following, although use of the library function, strcpy(), would be preferred:

```
void insertName(Person *aPerson, char *name)
{
    char *ptr = aPerson->name;

    while(*name != '\0')
    {
        *ptr = *name;
        ptr++; name++;
    }
    *ptr = '\0';
}
```

Some programmers use the [] notation to indicate that an array is to be used and the pointer notation to indicate a single quantity:

```
void    insertName(Person *, char []);
```

Whatever style is used for the function prototype and heading, it does not matter whether pointers or subscripts are used, in the function body, to access the arrays.

7.7.2   Pointers to Constants and Constant Pointers

An alternative to this, which also provides improved control over the program, involves the judicious use of the keyword const:

```
void    insertName(Person  * const aPerson, const char *name);
```

This says that the pointer aPerson, will not be modified but that the structure to which it points may be modified; that the pointer name may be modified so that it could move along an array but that the character to which it points at any stage will not be altered.

Within the function, the following would now be illegal:

```
aPerson++;                          /* cannot change the pointer */
*name = '\A';                       /* cannot change what it points to */
```

If a function only needs to use the values contained within a single structure but does not need to alter them, we would normally pass it by value, thus giving the function a copy of the structure. However there are times when the structure is so large that we may not wish to bear the overhead of a call by value. Under these circumstances we could use const in both places:

```
void    printPerson(const Person * const aPerson);
```

This would ensure that neither the pointer aPerson nor the structure to which is points can be changed.

Program 7.4 finds the location of one string within another could have been written using functions.

Program 7.4   (to find a substring)
_____

```
#include <stdio.h>
#include <stdlib.h>
#include <string.h>

#define    MaxWord          256

char * find(const char * const subStr, const char *fullStr);

main()
{
    char message[]  = "will it work with this string";
    char            word[MaxWord];
    char            *here;

    while(gets(word)  != NULL)
    {
        if((here = find(word, message))  == NULL)
            printf("not found\n");
        else
            printf("found at position %d\n", here - message);
    }

    exit(EXIT_SUCCESS);
}

char * find(const char * const subStr, const char *fullStr)
{
    while(*fullStr != '\0' &&
            strncmp(fullStr, subStr, strlen(subStr)) != 0)
        fullStr++;

    return *fullStr == '\0' ? NULL : fullStr;
}
```
_____

The prototype for the function `find()` shows us that the first argument `subStr` will not be incremented nor will the character to which it points be modified. On the other hand the second argument `fullStr` may be incremented but the character to which it points at any time will not be modified.

7.8 Arrays and Structures

We can once more see a difference in interpretation between arrays and structures. Although each offers a way of aggregating data, the name of a structure represents the whole structure whereas the name of an array represents the address of its zeroth element. This means that structure assignment is possible, structure arguments are passed by value and functions can return structures. Array assignment is not possible; when an array name is used as an actual argument, the address of its zeroth element is passed by value to a pointer; functions cannot return arrays, although they can return pointers.

8

Storage Allocation

The purpose of this chapter is to discuss the mechanism and purpose of dynamic storage allocation, sometimes referred to as *memory allocation*. Before we can do this, we need to examine how storage is allocated for the variables which we declare. The purpose of variable definition is to give a name to each piece of storage we need. We can then access it directly or by means of a pointer. There is however the additional need to be able to allocate storage dynamically and because such storage will be unnamed it will only be possible to access it by pointers.

8.1 Storage Allocation for Variables

For most purposes the compiler and/or the linker allocates the pieces of storage in which we store data. Each piece has an identifier as set out when we declare variables. However the time when the storage is actually allocated is determined by the storage class of the variable; this can be:

- an internal automatic variable
- a formal argument to a function
- an internal static variable
- an external variable

We will consider each in turn.

8.1.1   Internal Automatic Variables

This is the default storage class for variables declared within a compound statement; storage is allocated at the point of declaration and is released when control leaves the enclosing compound statement:

```
    {
        int     anInteger;          /* storage allocated for anInteger */
        float   aFloat;             /* storage allocated for aFloat */

        /* executable statements */
        {
            int     innerInt;       /* storage allocated for innerInt */

            /* executable statements */
        }                           /* storage for innerInt released*/

        /* more executable statements */

    }                       /* storage for anInteger and aFloat released */
```

8.1.2 Formal Arguments to Functions

These are similar to internal automatic variables with storage allocated on entry to the function and released when control leaves the function. One difference is that each formal argument is initialised with the value of the corresponding actual argument whereas internal variables may be uninitialised.

8.1.3 Internal Static Variables

Is it sometimes desirable to preserve the value and thus the storage allocated to an internal variable between consecutive invocations of a function. This is achieved by prefixing the declaration of the variable by the keyword `static`.

Program 8.1 has a function which will print a heading on a page together with the page number. The variable `pageNumber` is local to the function `printHeading()` but because it has `static` storage class, its value is preserved from one call of the function to the next.

Program 8.1

```
#include <stdio.h>

void printHeading(const char *aHeading);

main()
{
    printHeading("The title page");
    printHeading("A general page");
    printHeading("The last page");
}

void printHeading(const char *aHeading)
{
    static int     pageNumber = 1;

    printf("%s\t\t\t\tPage %d\n", aHeading, pageNumber);
    pageNumber++;
}
```

Sample output

```
The title page          Page 1
A general page          Page 2
The last page           Page 3
```

Storage for internal static variables in allocated and initialised immediately prior to the execution of the program and is not released until the end of execution. On first entry to the function `printHeading()` the variable `pageNumber` already has the value 1 and is only changed by the incrementation.

8.1.4   External Variables

Variables declared outside the functions are classified as external and can, potentially, be accessed from any part of the program.

As in the case of internal static variables, storage is allocated immediately prior to program execution and is not released until the end of execution.

8.2   Dynamic Allocation of Storage

The time when storage is allocated and released for the above four categories of variables is determined by the language and controlled by the compiler and the linker.

There are times however when the programmer wishes to exercise more precise control. A group of functions in the standard library is provided for this purpose:

```
#include   <stdlib.h>

void * malloc(size_t size);
void * calloc(size_t n, size_t size);
void * realloc(void *ptr, size_t size);

void free(void *ptr);
```

The type `size_t` is defined in the header file `stddef.h` as the unsigned integral type which the operator `sizeof` produces. A typical entry in `stddef.h` will be:

```
typedef unsigned int size_t;
```

The function `malloc()` allocates space for an object of `size` bytes and returns a pointer to this object. If it is unable to allocate the requested space, it returns `NULL`. The return type is the generic pointer `void *` which must be cast to another pointer type before is can be used:

```
int    *ptr;
Person *refPerson;

ptr = (int *) malloc(sizeof(int));        /* allocate space for an int */
if(ptr == NULL)
{
    printf("out of storage\n");
    exit(EXIT_FAILURE);
}
else
{
    *ptr = 37;
    ...
}


                                         /* allocate space for a Person */
if((refPerson = (Person *)malloc(sizeof(Person))) == NULL)
{
    printf("out of storage\n");
    exit(EXIT_FAILURE);
}
else
{
    refPerson->age = 18;
    ...
}
```

It is commonplace to use the `sizeof` operator to determine the size of the object for which space is to be allocated. The return value from `malloc()` needs to be cast appropriately and it is good practice to test that `malloc()` was successful.

At some later stage in the program but not necessarily in the function which calls `malloc()`, the space for the object can be released by:

```
free(refPerson);
free(ptr);
```

The pointer passed to `free()` must contain a value which originated from one of the functions `malloc()`, `calloc()` or `realloc()`. It would be acceptable but unnecessary to cast the actual argument to `free()`:

```
free((void *)refPerson);
```

The function `calloc()` allocates space for an array of n elements each of `size` bytes. A most important difference from `malloc()` is that `calloc()` initialises the allocated space to zeroes whereas `malloc()` leaves the space uninitialised. With these points in mind there is a certain amount of interchangeability between the two:

```
                        /* an array of 20 Persons initialised to zeros */
refPerson = (Person *)calloc(20, sizeof(Person));

                           /* an unitialised array of 20 Persons */
refPerson = (Person *)malloc(20*sizeof(Person));

                        /* a single Person initialised to zeros */
```

```
refPerson = (Person *)calloc(1, sizeof(Person));

                                    /* a single uninitialised Person */
refPerson = (Person *)malloc(sizeof(Person));
```

Once space for an array has been allocated, it can be accessed in the usual ways by subscript or pointer:

```
Person *refPerson;
Person *thisOne;
int     index;

refPerson = (Person *)calloc(20, sizeof(Person));
if(refPerson == NULL)
    exit(EXIT_FAILURE);

for(index = 0; index<20; index++)
    process(refPerson[index]);

for(thisOne = refPerson; thisone < refPerson + 20; thisOne++)
    process(*thisOne);
```

The function `realloc()` changes the size of the object to which `ptr` points and allocates `size` bytes which may be larger or smaller than that originally allocated. It may simply be able to extend the currently allocated space or may allocate a new piece of space of the required size. Whatever it does, it returns a pointer to this space or `NULL` if it cannot allocate.

The orginal contents of the space are preserved, being copied if necessary. Any extra space that is requested is uninitialised. If the value of `ptr` is `NULL`, `realloc()` has the same effect as `malloc()`.

8.3 Dynamic Data Structures

8.3.1 A Linked List

Although arrays and `structs` are provided by the language to help us group data in meaningful ways they are not always the most appropriate data structures to use. More general arrangements which provide greater flexibility can be constructed from linked lists. Ideally a data structure is defined by the operations it can perform. For example, if we can only add items to the structure and remove items from the structure and furthermore if the only item we can remove at any stage is the latest one we have added, then we have what is commonly called a stack. More general structures enable us to add and/or remove items at the front, the back or any place in the middle. The items in the structure may be sorted according to some criterion such that whenever we add a new item it finds its correct place.

A common means of implementing some of these types of collection is a linked list which may be singly or double linked. In a single linked list, each item knows which item follows it whereas in a doubly linked list each item knows which item precedes it as well.

We will consider a singly linked list representing a queue. In this, new members are added only to the back and removals take place only from the front. Two structures are needed:

member   which contains two pointers, the first to the next member and the second to some data

queue   which notes the front and back members together with the number of members currently present

It is not really necessary to have the pointer back nor the variable number but they are useful. The data could be of any type: an int, a double, a Person structure etc. A typical queue would appear as:

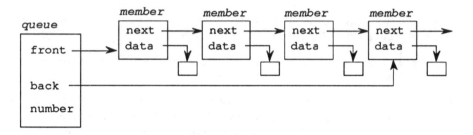

The definitions for the two structures would be:

```
typedef struct X {
                struct X   *next;
                someType   *data;
            }
                member;

typedef struct    {
                member *front;
                member *back;
                int     number;
            }
                queue;
```

We have used an arbitrary tag X for the first structure since it is only needed for the declaration of the pointer next. Once we have completed the typedef we will simply use the type member. An alternative approach is to declare what we mean by member before we define struct X, enabling us to use member within the definition:

```
typedef struct X member;

typedef struct X {
                member     *next;
                someType   *data;
            }
                member;
```

The type `someType` has been left arbitrary at this stage and will need to be `typedef`'d onto some specific type such as:

```
typedef    int    someType;
typedef    Person someType;
```

The functions we will need to handle the general queue mechanisms independently of the details of the specific type are:

- to create a new `queue` object; this will need to allocate storage for the queue object and initialise it appropriately:

  ```
  queue *newQueue(void);
  ```

- to add a data value to the end of a given queue; this will create a new `member` object to contain the data value and then append it to the queue:

  ```
  void add(someType *dataValue, queue *aQueue);
  ```

- to remove the first item from a given queue; this will take the first `member` from the queue, extract the data value, release the storage for the `member` casing and return a pointer to the data value:

  ```
  someType *removeFirst(queue *aQueue);
  ```

- to join, or concatenate, one queue onto the back of another:

  ```
  queue *queueCat(queue *thisQueue, queue *thatQueue);
  ```

- to return a pointer to the first data value but not to remove it from the queue:

  ```
  someType *first(queue *aQueue);
  ```

- to report how many members there are in a queue:

  ```
  int size(queue *aQueue);
  ```

- to indicate whether a queue is empty or not:

  ```
  boolean empty(queue *aQueue);
  ```

- to print the contents of a queue; this scans the members of the queue calling, for each, another function which will print the data value:

  ```
  void printQueue(char * message, queue *aQueue);
  ```

  The function to print the data itself will be specific to the type of data:

  ```
  void printData(someType *dataValue);
  ```

Putting all these together and including `const` in the appropriate places we have the following set of declarations and prototypes. No argument points to an array and so each one is a constant pointer such as `queue  *const aQueue;` many functions do not attempt to alter the object to which the argument points and so these arguments are pointers to constants such as `const queue *const aQueue.`

Program 8.2 (part 1)

```
#include  <stdio.h>
#include  <stdlib.h>

typedef   enum {false, true} boolean;

typedef   int    someType;                    /* for illustration */

typedef struct X member;

typedef struct X {
              member    *next;
              someType  *data;
         }
              member;

typedef struct   {
              member *front;
              member *back;
              int    number;
         }
              queue;

/* ---------------------------------------------------------------
Prototypes:      Independent of the details of someType
---------------------------------------------------------------- */
queue *   newQueue(void);

void      add(const someType *const dataValue, queue *const aQueue);
someType * removeFirst(queue *const aQueue);
queue *   queueCat(queue *const thisQueue, queue *const thatQueue);

someType * first(const queue *const aQueue);

boolean   empty(const queue *const aQueue);
int       size(const queue *const aQueue);

void      printQueue(const char *const message,
              const queue *const aQueue);

/* ---------------------------------------------------------------
Prototypes:      Background functions
---------------------------------------------------------------- */
member *  newMember(const someType *const dataValue);
void      outOfStorage(void);
```

The functions which allocate storage are `newQueue()` and `newMember()`. Because we have used `calloc()` instead of `malloc()`, the queue structure needs no specific initialisation. Nevertheless we regard it as good practice to encapsulate this activity within a function. If other initialisation were needed, this is where it would be placed.

The creation of a `member` object needs a data value which is presented to the function `newMember()` as an argument. Here we see that more work is needed; space is allocated to hold the data value and then the data value itself is copied into this space.

Program 8.2 (part 2)

```
/* -----------------------------------------------------------------
create a new queue, intialized to zero
------------------------------------------------------------- */
queue *   newQueue(void)
{
    queue *aQueue = (queue *) calloc(1, sizeof(queue));

    if(aQueue == NULL)
       outOfStorage();
    else
       return aQueue;
}

/* -----------------------------------------------------------------
create a new member to contain dataValue
------------------------------------------------------------- */
member *newMember(const someType *const dataValue)
{
    member *result;
                                    /* create space for a member */
    result = (member *)calloc(1, sizeof(member));
    if(result == NULL)
       outOfStorage();
                                    /* create space for the data */
    result->data = (someType *)calloc(1, sizeof(someType));
    if(result->data == NULL)
       outOfStorage();
                              /* copy the data into the space */
    *(result->data) = *dataValue;

    return result;
}

/* -----------------------------------------------------------------
exit tidily when out of storage
------------------------------------------------------------- */
void outOfStorage(void)
{
    fprintf(stderr,"Out of storage\n");
    exit(EXIT_FAILURE);
}
```

The next group of functions simply report features of the queue such as its current size, whether it is empty, its first data value or print all the data values in the queue. This latter operation is handled by two functions: `printQueue()` scans the queue, regardless of the type of data stored in it but calls `printData()` which is specific to the type of data.

Program 8.2 (part 3)
```
/* ------------------------------------------------------------------
return the size of aQueue
----------------------------------------------------------- */
int    size(const queue *const aQueue){
    return aQueue->number;
}

/* ------------------------------------------------------------------
indicate whether aQueue is empty or not
----------------------------------------------------------- */
boolean    empty(const queue *const aQueue){
    return aQueue->number == 0;
}

/* ------------------------------------------------------------------
return the data value in the first member of aQueue, do not remove it
----------------------------------------------------------- */
someType * first(const queue *const aQueue){
    if(empty(aQueue))
        return NULL;
    else
        return aQueue->front->data;
}

/* ------------------------------------------------------------------
display details of aQueue
----------------------------------------------------------- */
void printQueue(const char *const message, const queue *const aQueue)
{
    member *thisOne;

    printf("\n%s with %d members: ", message, size(aQueue));
    for(thisOne = aQueue->front; thisOne != NULL;
                                  thisOne = thisOne->next)
        printData(thisOne->data);
    putchar('\n');
}

/* ------------------------------------------------------------------
display the data value
    specific to the fact that someType is typedefed onto int in this
    program
----------------------------------------------------------- */
void printData(const someType *const dataValue){
    printf("[%d] ", *dataValue);
}
```

Next come the functions which do the real work of managing the queue: add()
places a new data value onto the back of the queue and removeFirst() takes the
first data value from the queue.

A typical situation before a new data value is added would be:

Before adding a new data value:

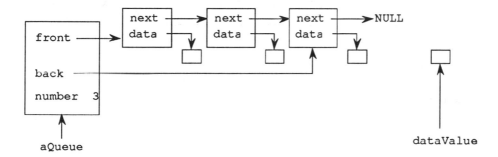

```
/* -----------------------------------------------------------------
add a dataValue to back of aQueue, creating a new member for the data
--------------------------------------------------------------- */
void add(const someType *const dataValue, queue *const aQueue)
{
    if(empty(aQueue))
        aQueue->front = aQueue->back = newMember(dataValue);
    else
    {
        aQueue->back->next = newMember(dataValue);
        aQueue->back       = aQueue->back->next;
    }

    aQueue->number++;
}
```

After the data value has been added:

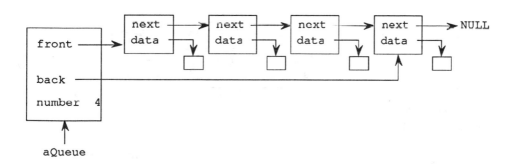

Removing the first data value gives rise to the following:

Before a data value is removed:

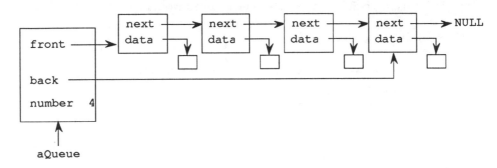

```
/* ----------------------------------------------------------------
remove the first member from aQueue, return its data value
--------------------------------------------------------------- */
someType *    removeFirst(queue *const aQueue)
{
    if(empty(aQueue))
        return NULL;
    else
    {
        member    *thisOne = aQueue->front;
        someType  *result;

        aQueue->front = thisOne->next;
        if(--aQueue->number == 0)
            aQueue->back = NULL;

        result = thisOne->data;            /* note the data value */
        free(thisOne);               /* get rid of the member casing */

        return result;
    }
}
```

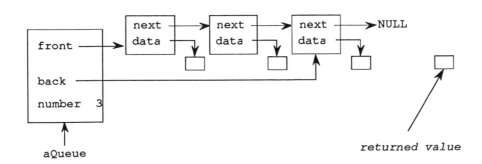

returned value

Finally, the function to join one queue to another and a sample program to illustrate the use of this group of functions.

Program 8.2 (part 4)

```
/* --------------------------------------------------------------
join thisQueue onto the back of thatQueue
---------------------------------------------------------- */
queue *       queueCat(queue *const thisQueue, queue *const thatQueue)
{
    if (empty(thisQueue))
        return thatQueue;
    else if (!empty(thatQueue))
    {
        thisQueue->back->next = thatQueue->front;
        thisQueue->back       = thatQueue->back;
        thisQueue->number    += thatQueue->number;

        thatQueue->front  = thatQueue->back = NULL;
        thatQueue->number = 0;

    }
    return thisQueue;
}



/* --------------------------------------------------------------
a sample program to illustrate some of the features
---------------------------------------------------------- */
main()
{
    queue      *firstQueue;
    queue      *secondQueue;
                    /* this program has typedefed someType onto int */
    someType   data;

    firstQueue = newQueue();
    secondQueue = newQueue();

    printf("Enter values for the first queue (end with zero):\n");
    while(scanf("%d", &data), data != 0)
        add(&data, firstQueue);

    printQueue("First Queue", firstQueue);

    printf("The first value is %d\n", *(first(firstQueue)));

    printf("Enter values for the second queue (end with zero):\n");
    while(scanf("%d", &data), data != 0)
        add(&data, secondQueue);

    printQueue("Second Queue", secondQueue);
```

```
        printf("First two values removed: %d ",
                              *(removeFirst(secondQueue)));
        printf("%d\n", *(removeFirst(secondQueue)));

        printQueue("New second queue", secondQueue);

        queueCat(firstQueue, secondQueue);
        printQueue("First Queue", firstQueue);
        printQueue("Second Queue", secondQueue);

        exit(EXIT_SUCCESS);
}
```

Sample input(in bold) and output)
_____

Enter values for the first queue (end with zero):
12
34
45
65
0

First Queue with 4 members: [12] [34] [45] [65]
The first value is 12
Enter values for the second queue (end with zero):
234
543
654
876
677
0

Second Queue with 5 members: [234] [543] [654] [876] [677]
First two values removed: 234 543

New second queue with 3 members: [654] [876] [677]

First Queue with 7 members: [12] [34] [45] [65] [654] [876] [677]

Second Queue with 0 members:
_____

8.3.2   Dynamically Sized Arrays

In addition to declaring arrays in the usual way, we can use `calloc()` to allocate space for use as an array and we can then use `realloc()` to alter its size during the execution of the program.

We wish to store an unknown number of character strings in an array. A common approach would be to decide that since a character string is stored in a character array, a two dimensional array is needed. We would have to estimate how many strings our program should accommodate and test that we do not try to accept more than this. Furthermore we would have to estimate the length of the longest string to set the other dimension of our array:

```
char    table[maxStringLength][numberOfStrings]
```

If, as is likely, many strings are much shorter than maxStringLength, much space will be wasted.

An alternative approach is to use one sufficiently large one-dimensional array into which we place, in turn, each new string from the input stream. We can then measure the length of each string and allocate space for it. To keep all the strings together we need an array of pointers where each element of the array points to a different string. If we allocate the space for this dynamically, we can extend it as and when necessary.

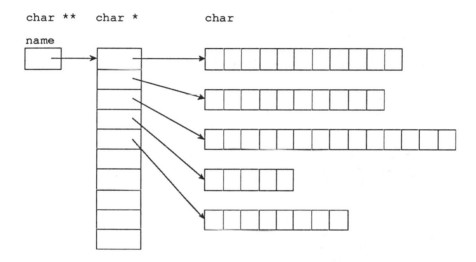

We need only one variable, name. This points to the array of pointers each element of which points to a character. We thus have an array of char to hold each character string, and array of char * to hold the pointers to them. The variable name which points to the first element of this array therefore needs to be of type char **.

Program 8.3 reads lines of text from the input stream into the character array buffer which has been set to an arbitrarily large size. The constant BUFSIZ (note the spelling!) is defined in stdio.h and is useful for these purposes. The length of this character string is measured with strlen() and the correct amount of space for the string is allocated with malloc(). Note that we must make allowance for the terminating null character.

Before we do this we need to ensure that the array of pointers to which name points is large enough. If it is not, it needs to be extended by using realloc(). The variable size represents the current size of this array which grows in chunks according to the constant chunk. The variable index is set to the next array element which needs to be used and thus indicates how many entries there are at any time.

Program 8.3

```c
#include <stdio.h>
#include <stdlib.h>
#include <string.h>

#define    chunk   4

void outOfStorage(void);

main()
{
    char    buffer[BUFSIZ];
    char    **name = NULL;
    int     size  = 0;
    int     index = 0;

    while(printf("Text: "), gets(buffer) != NULL)
    {
        if(index >= size)
        {
            size += chunk;                    /* increase the array size */

                                              /* extend the array */
            name = (char **)realloc(name, size * sizeof(char *));
            if(name == NULL)
                outOfStorage();
        }

                        /* allocate space for the current string */
        name[index] = (char *)malloc(strlen(buffer) + 1);
        if(name[index] == NULL)
            outOfStorage();

                    /* copy the current string into the new space */
        strcpy(name[index], buffer);
        index++;
    }

                                            /* some trial output */
    printf("Text in reverse order: %d entries:\n\n", index);
    while(--index >= 0)
        puts(name[index]);

    putchar('\n');

    exit(EXIT_SUCCESS);
}


void outOfStorage(void)
{
    fprintf(stderr,"Out of storage\n");
    exit(EXIT_FAILURE);
}
```

Sample input(in bold) and output

```
Text: the first line entered
Text: another piece of text
Text: yet one more for luck
Text: this is the last to be entered
Text:

Text in reverse order: 4 entries:

this is the last to be entered
yet one more for luck
another piece of text
the first line entered
```

When the program starts, both size and index are set to zero. When the first string is read in, the array of pointers needs to be set up. The function realloc() is used here and because name has the value NULL, it acts in the same way as a call to malloc().

The program then simply outputs the strings in reverse order to show that it had stored them correctly.

8.4 Functions Returning Pointers

We have now seen a number of examples of functions which return pointers. This is perfectly straightforward as long as we ensure the we return the address of a piece of storage that remains in existence after we have returned from the function.

We must not return a pointer to an automatic variable which is local to the called function. Legitimate storage locations can be created by making the local variable static or by creating the space dynamically or by leaving the responsibility to the calling function.

Program 8.4 illustrates all these approaches. Each variant of the function prompts the user to input the day , month and year of a date. We use the string handling function gets() to read a line of input. In the case of the day and the year which are to be stored as integers we also use the library function atoi() which converts an ASCII string to integer. Note that, in common with other string handling functions, gets() returns a pointer to its argument buffer; this enables us to use this return value as the argument of atoi().

Program 8.4

```
#include <stdio.h>
#include <stdlib.h>
#include <string.h>

#define   maxMonth  10
typedef struct{
                int     day;
                char    month[maxMonth];
                int     year;
            }
                date;

date *getDateLocal(void);
date *getDateArg(date * const aDate);
date *getDateStatic(void);
date *getDateMalloc(void);
void printDate(date aDate);

main()
{
    date someDate;                      /* some actual space */
    date *ptrDate;                    /* pointer to nowhere yet */

    ptrDate = getDateLocal();
    printDate(*ptrDate);

    ptrDate = getDateArg(&someDate);
    printDate(*ptrDate);

    ptrDate = getDateStatic();
    printDate(*ptrDate);

    ptrDate = getDateMalloc();
    printDate(*ptrDate);

    exit(EXIT_SUCCESS);
}

/* ------------------------------------------------------------
    returns a pointer to an automatic local variable
    this is incorrect
------------------------------------------------------------- */
date *getDateLocal(void)
{
    char    buffer[80];
    date    localDate;

    printf("Day:    "); localDate.day = atoi(gets(buffer));
    printf("Month:  "); gets(localDate.month);
    printf("Year:   "); localDate.year = atoi(gets(buffer));
```

```c
/* ----------------------------------------------------------------
   returns a copy of its argument
   ------------------------------------------------------------ */
date *getDateArg(date * const aDate)
{
    char    buffer[80];

    printf("Day:    "); aDate->day = atoi(gets(buffer));
    printf("Month: "); gets(aDate->month);
    printf("Year:   "); aDate->year = atoi(gets(buffer));

    return aDate;
}
/* ----------------------------------------------------------------
   returns a pointer to an internal static variable
   ------------------------------------------------------------ */
date *getDateStatic(void)
{
    char         buffer[80];
    static date  staticDate;

    printf("Day:    "); staticDate.day = atoi(gets(buffer));
    printf("Month: "); gets(staticDate.month);
    printf("Year:   "); staticDate.year = atoi(gets(buffer));

    return &staticDate;
}

/* ----------------------------------------------------------------
   returns a pointer to dynamically allocated storage
   ------------------------------------------------------------ */
date *getDateMalloc(void)
{
    char    buffer[80];
    date    *ptrDate = (date *)malloc(sizeof(date));

    printf("Day:    "); ptrDate->day = atoi(gets(buffer));
    printf("Month: "); gets(ptrDate->month);
    printf("Year:   "); ptrDate->year = atoi(gets(buffer));

    return ptrDate;
}

void printDate(date aDate)
{
    printf("%d %s %d\n", aDate.day, aDate.month, aDate.year);
}
```

In each case, we have used the object to which ptrDate points as the argument to the printDate() function. getDateLocal() is incorrect in that when control has returned to main() the space allocated to the local variable to which we are still pointing can be reallocated for other use. The three other variants are all acceptable but some care needs to be taken with each.

that there is no need to return a pointer to this, which is true; however we gain the same advantage as we have with the `gets()` function. The return value can be used in another expression.

Whenever `getDateStatic()` is called its return value always points to the same piece of storage. Even though the storage remains allocated after the return, care is needed in the following set of circumstances:

```
date    *ptr1;
date    *ptr2;

ptr1 = getDateStatic();
ptr2 = getDateStatic();
```

At this stage, both pointers point to the same space and so `*ptr1` and `*ptr2` yield the same value.

`getDateMalloc()` creates a new piece of space every time it is called. This overcomes the last problem but now the caller of this function has the responsibility for releasing this space when it is no longer needed:

```
date    *ptr;

ptr = getDateMalloc();
printDate(*ptr);
ptr = getDateMalloc();
```

The space to which `ptr` pointed after the first call to `getDateMalloc()` has now been left stranded. We should have included `free(ptr)` before the second call.

9

Character Strings

We have already noted that the language provides no special facilities for handling strings of characters. All useful activities such as input and output of strings, comparison, concatenation and copying are performed by functions in the standard library

Strings are stored in arrays of type char and it is the responsibility of the programmer to declare these to be a suitable size. The string itself may occupy less space than the size of the array which holds it and can change in length during the course of execution. The array, on the other hand, has a fixed length.

There are two methods commonly used by languages to note the length of a character string. One is to have a hidden integer value, recording how many characters are in the string; the other is to have a special character as the last character of the string. C adopts this latter approach. This terminating character is the null character '\0' i.e. the character with ASCII value zero. All the string handling functions in the standard library adopt this terminator and when we use string constants in the language a null character is automatically appended. There are however times when the programmer is responsible for ensuring that the null character is correctly placed.

9.1 Declaring and Initialising Strings

Space is allocated for strings in the usual manner when we declare the necessary arrays. A variety of possibilities in illustrated in Program 9.1. An array may be initialised as an ordinary array of characters, as shown by string2[]; a special, more convenient form is also provided, as shown by string3[] and string4[].

Program 9.1

```
#include <stdio.h>

main ()
{
                                /* unitialised array of 8 characters */
    char    string1[8];

                /* array of 8 characters initialised in standard way */
    char    string2[8] = {'h', 'e', 'l', 'l', 'o', '\0'};

                /* array of 8 characters initialised in alternative way */
    char    string3[8] = "hello";

                            /* intialised array of sufficient size */
    char    string4[]   = "hello";

                            /* pointer initialised to point to a string */
    char    *string5    = "hello";

    printf("size of arrays:\n");
    printf("\t\t\tstring3   %d characters\n", sizeof(string3));
    printf("\t\t\tstring4   %d characters\n", sizeof(string4));
}
```

Sample output

```
size of arrays:
            string3   8 characters
            string4   6 characters
```

The layout in memory of the last three strings in Program 9.1 would be as:

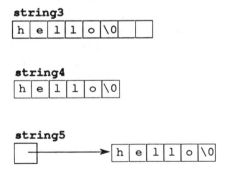

string1 is an unitialised array of char ready for use. string2 is another, initialised in the way common to all arrays; when using this approach, the programmer is responsible for including the terminating null. string3 uses the alternative, more common, form for initialising strings. For string4, the size of the array is not specified; only space for the initialising string is allocated, namely six characters as is demonstrated by the output from the program. string5 is different in that it is a pointer which happens to be initialised to point to a string. It can be re-used to point to any other character which may or may not be in an array; for the others, their contents may be changed but they will remain character arrays of the declared sizes.

9.2 Header File

When using any of the string handling functions from the standard library it is necessary to include the header file string.h:

```
#include <string.h>
```

This contains all the prototypes for the functions.

9.3 A First Set of Functions

The most commonly used group of string handling functions is:

Copying
```
        char    *strcpy(char *destination, const char *source);
```

Concatenating
```
        char    *strcat(char *destination, const char *source);
```

Comparing
```
        int     strcmp(const char *stringA, const char *stringB);
```

Length of string
```
        size_t  strlen(const char *aString);
```

It is assumed that each argument to these functions points to an array of characters.

In strcpy(), source is copied to destination; any previous contents of destination are lost. strcat() acts in a similar manner except that the contents of source are appended to the end of the contents of destination. The terminating null of destination is removed and a new one is placed at the new end after the concatentation. In both cases it is your responsibility to make destination large enough to hold the result.

strcmp() compares the two strings presented to it and returns:

a negative value	if stringA comes before stringB in the sorting sequence
zero	if they are identical
a positive value	if stringA comes after stringB

Do not assume that the values returned are necessarily −1, 0 and +1; the Standard only requires negative and positive values for non-equality.

strlen() returns the number of characters in aString; the terminating null is not regarded as part of the string. The type size_t is defined in the header file stddef.h as the unsigned integral type which the operator sizeof produces. A typical entry in stddef.h will be:

```
typedef unsigned int size_t;
```

Examples:

```
char    date[30];
char    day[10] = "Monday";
char    today[] = "Tuesday";
char    *ptr = "message";
int     length;

strcpy(day, today);                 /* day contains: Tuesday */
strcpy(day, "Wednesday");           /* day contains: Wesnesday */
strcpy(day, ptr);                   /* day contains: message */

strcpy(date, "Monday");             /* date contains: Monday */
strcat(date, ", 13 January");
                        /* date contains: Monday, 13 January */

strcpy(day, "Sunday");
if(strcmp(day, date) < 0) ...      /* does day come before date? */
if(strcmp(day, "Monday") == 0) ../* does day contain "Monday"? */

length = strlen(day);               /* length has value:  6 */
length = strlen(date);              /* length has value: 18 */
```

Why do `strcpy()` and `strcat()` return a `char *` and to which character does this point? Each function returns the value of `destination`. This enables us to use the function as part of another expression if we so wish. In the above, we could have combined the copying of `"Sunday"` into `day` with the subsequent `strcmp()`:

```
if(strcmp(strcpy(day, "Sunday"), date) < 0) ...
```

9.3.1   Restricting the Action

Related to this group of functions is another:

Copying
```
char *strncpy(char *destination, const char *source, size_t nChars);
```

Concatenating
```
char *strncat(char *destination, const char *source, size_t nChars);
```

Comparing
```
int  strncmp(const char *stringA, const char *stringB, size_t nChars);
```

Note the letter `'n'` which has been slipped into the middle of each function name together with the additional parameter. The activity of each function is now restricted to the first nChars characters of `source`. This means that, for copying and concatenating, if `source` contains more than nChars characters, only the first nChars are copied to `destination`. One consequence is that the terminating null will not be copied. It is your responsibility to ensure that `destination` is terminated correctly. If `source` contains fewer than nChars characters, the effect is the same as in the corresponding `strcpy()` and `strcat()` functions.

9.4 Input and Output of Strings

Two useful functions, one to obtain a string from standard input and the other to output one to standard output are:

String input
```
char    *gets(char *aString);
```

String output
```
int     puts(const char *aString);
```

When using either of these, include the header file:

```
#include <stdio.h>
```

gets() assumes that aString is pointing to an array large enough to accept the input; it reads characters from the standard input until the return character is entered, placing the characters in this array. The return character is not placed in the array but a terminating null is appended. The function returns the value of aString, unless it encounters the end of file in which case it returns NULL.

puts() copies the character to which aString points and subsequent characters to the standard output, stopping only when it encounters a null character. This is replaced, on the output, by a return character. If a write error occurs, it returns the constant EOF otherwise it returns a non-negative value.

9.5 An Example

Program 9.2 maintains a sorted array of character strings. Strings are read from standard input and inserted into an array which always maintains its ordering.

The main part of the program declares an array of strings, name, to store a collection of names; a variable, newName, which will store each name as it is entered; a variable, nEntries, to note how many names have been stored in the array. We have used a typedef to define string; this hides the fact that we really have a two-dimensional array of characters. In this program it is more convenient to think of a one-dimensional array of strings.

The while loop prompts the user for a name, accepting it into the string newName and then tests the return value of gets() to determine whether a string was entered or not. If it were, the function addName() is called to do the real work.

The array, name, stores the individual names in ascending order. When a new name arrives, the array is scanned from the beginning to find out where the new one should be placed. If it needs to go at the end it is simply appended to the array, otherwise those that are to come after it are moved up the array and the new one in inserted.

Program 9.2
_____

```c
#include <stdio.h>
#include <string.h>

#define    listMax    100
#define    stringMax  80

typedef enum {false, true} boolean;
typedef char string[stringMax];

void addName(string *name, string newOne, int *listSize);
void printNames(string *name, int listSize);

main()
{
    string newName;              /* a place to store a new string */
    string name[listMax];        /* an array of strings */
    int    nEntries = 0;

    while(printf("Name: %d: ", nEntries), gets(newName) != NULL)
        addName(name, newName, &nEntries);

    printNames(name, nEntries);
}


/* ------------------------------------------------------------
    adds a new string, newOne, to an array of strings, name
    updates the number in the array: listSize
----------------------------------------------------------- */
void addName(string *name, string newOne, int *listSize)
{
    if(*listSize >= listMax)
        return;                              /* the array is full */
    else
    {
        int        k = 0;
        boolean    found = false;
                            /* search for the place for newOne */
        while(!found && k < *listSize)
            found = strcmp(newOne, name[k++]) < 0;

        k--;                                 /* move back one place */

        if(found)
        {
            int    j;
                    /* move the tail along to make room for newOne */
```

```
            (*listSize)++;                      /* one more in the list */
        }

        return;
    }


    void    printNames(string *name, int listSize)
    {
        int     k;

        printf("\nNumber of Entries: %d\n\n", listSize);
        for(k = 0; k < listSize; k++)
            puts(name[k]);
    }
```

Sample input(in bold) and output

```
Name:  0:  Charles⏎
Name:  1:  Juliet⏎
Name:  2:  James⏎
Name:  3:  Frederick⏎
Name:  4:  Walter⏎
Name:  5:  Barbara⏎
Name:  6:  Nicholas⏎
Name:  7:  ⏎

Number of Entries: 7

Barbara
Charles
Frederick
James
Juliet
Nicholas
Walter
```

9.6 Searching for Characters

Another group of functions enables us to search a string for a given character:

Left-most character
```
char    *strchr (const char *aString, int aChar);
```

Right-most character
```
char    *strrchr(const char *aString, int aChar);
```

Substring
```
char    *strstr(const char *aString, const char *subString);
```

The first two functions search the string to which aString points for an occurrence of aChar; strchr() searches for the left-most occurrence and strrchr()

searches for the right-most occurrence. If such an occurrence is found, each function returns a pointer to it, otherwise it returns NULL.

The function strstr() searches aString from the left, looking for an occurrence of subString. If it is successful, it returns a pointer to the start of the sub-string that it has found, otherwise it returns NULL.

Program 9.3 illustrates the use of these functions. When reading individual characters, one would expect to use the function getchar() but the return character then has to be handled separately. We have consumed a complete input line, including the return character, with gets() and then used just the first character, subString[0]. The position of the character in the main string is found by pointer arithmetic.

Program 9.3

```c
#include <stdio.h>
#include <string.h>

main()
{
    char    message[] = "A trial string for searching";
    char    subString[80];
    char    *leftMost;
    char    *rightMost;
    char    *location;

    printf("The test string is: <%s>\n\n", message);
    puts("\nSearching for a Character\n");

    while(printf("A character: "), strcmp(gets(subString)," ") != 0)
    {
        if((leftMost = strchr(message, subString[0])) == NULL)
            puts("Not found");
        else
        {
            rightMost = strrchr(message, subString[0]);
            printf("Found: left-most position: %d ",
                                        leftMost - message);
            printf("right-most position: %d\n",
                                        rightMost - message);
        }
    }

    puts("\nSearching for a sub-string\n");
    while(printf("A string: "), gets(subString) != NULL)
    {
        if((location = strstr(message, subString)) == NULL)
            puts("Not found");
        else
            printf("Found <%s> at location: %d\n",
                                    subString, location - message);
    }
}
```

Sample input(in bold) and output

```
The test string is: <A trial string for searching>


Searching for a Character

A character: s⏎
Found: left-most position: 8 right-most position: 19
A character: g⏎
Found: left-most position: 13 right-most position: 27
A character: l⏎
Found: left-most position: 6 right-most position: 6
A character: p⏎
Not found
A character: ⏎


Searching for a sub-string

A string: tri⏎
Found <tri> at location: 2
A string: A tri⏎
Found <A tri> at location: 0
A string: ing for⏎
Found <ing for> at location: 11
A string: extra⏎
Not found
A string: ⏎
```

9.7 Program Arguments

The main function of a program, main(), is like any other function in all respects except three. We cannot call it from another function: it is activated automatically as the first function when program execution begins. If and when we return from it, we terminate execution of the program. We have limited choice about its arguments: it can either have no arguments or two arguments:

```
int main()                              /* no arguments */

int main(int argc, char *argv[])        /* two arguments */
```

It is this second form that we will now explore. The actual arguments are provided when we execute the program from the command line of the operating system. If our source code is in a file called sort.c, we would create the executable form by calling the C compiler such as:

```
cc -o sort sort.c
```

which, on a Unix, system would create an executable file called `program`. On an MS-DOS system, the executable file would be called `program.exe`. On either system we would run the program by simply typing the command:

```
sort                                    /* no arguments */

sort -r data-file results-file          /* with arguments */
```

Inside `main()`, `argc` tells us how many arguments have been presented and `argv` is a pointer to an array of pointers, each element of which points to the first character of an argument. For the second use of the `sort` program the layout of the arguments would be:

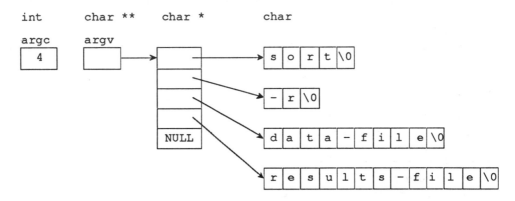

In this case we can see, from `argc`, that there are four arguments. `argv` points to an array whose zeroth element points to the program name itself and whose last element is `NULL`. Each of its other elements points to a null-terminated character array. The program is now free to interpret these characters strings in any way it wishes.

The Progam 9.4 simply reports the number and content of each of its arguments.

Program 9.4

```c
#include  <stdio.h>

int main(int argc, char *argv[])
{
    int    index;

    printf("number of arguments: %d \n\n", argc);

    for(index = 0; index<argc; index++)
        printf("argument: %d: [%s]\n", index, argv[index]);
}
```

Sample output (assuming the program is called sort)

```
number of arguments: 4

argument: 0: [sort]
argument: 1: [-r]
argument: 2: [data-file]
argument: 3: [results-file]
```

Equipped with the ability to access arrays by means of pointers, alternatives are available for processing the program arguments:

```
                    /* loop controlled by the number of arguments */
  while(--argc > 0)
    process(*++argv);                /* *argv is of type char *  */


                /* loop controlled by the contents of the element
                    to which argv points, being non-NULL  */
  while(*++argv != NULL)
    process(*argv);
```

In each case the function process() needs to be declared to be:

```
  void process(char *);
```

There is nothing sacrosanct about the identifiers argc and argv. Although it has been the convention to use them, any names are permissible since they are local to main():

```
  int main(int nArguments, char * argument[]);
```

10

Program Structure

In the programs we have examined so far, we have assumed that all the source code is in one file. When we develop large programs it is useful to be able to sub-divide them into logical units each of which is in its own source file. This offers the twin advantages of separate compilation and improved control over the scope and visibility of functions and variables.variables:scope of

Variables can be arranged to be:

a)   global to the whole program and thus available to all functions in all the files

b)   local to one file and thus available only to the functions in that file

c)   local to a compound statement

d)   local to a function; a direct consequence of c)

Functions can be arranged to be:

a)   global to the whole program and thus available to all functions in all the files

b)   local to one file and thus available only to the functions in that file

In this chapter we will examine these issues, noting the difference in meaning between definition and declaration of identifiers; seeing how to control the scope of identifiers; and examining the rules governing the initialisation of variables.

10.1　Multi-file Programs

In its simplest form, a program is a collection of functions and external variables. In contrast to some other languages it is not possible, in C, to nest one function inside another in order to restrict its visibility. The only way in which we can group functions into logical or related groups is by placing them into separate files.

It is usually easier to maintain a program when it is split into a number of separate files than when it is all contained within a single file. Since the process of compilation takes some time, it is preferable to compile a small file than a large one. When an error occurs, recompilation of only that file which needs to be modified is quicker than recompiling the complete source code.

The creation of an executable file from one or more source files requires two steps:

i)　　compilation of each source file into a corresponding object file

ii)　　linking the object files and any libraries together to form the executable file

The precise way in which this is achieved differs from one operating system to anther. On a Unix system, source files have names which end in .c and their corresponding objects files bear the same basic name but end in .o . The executable file can have any name. Suppose that we are creating an editor, named edit. The source has been created in source files: interface.c, io.c, search.c and block.c. The following command would produce an object file named interface.o:

```
cc -c interface.c
```

All the object files could be created by one command:

```
cc -c interface.c io.c search.c block.c
```

To create an executable file named edit we can present a mixture of source files (.c) and object files (.o) and tell the compiler by means of the -o flag that the executable file should be called edit:

```
cc -o edit interface.c io.c search.o block.o
```

Once we have an executable file, this can be used:

```
edit aDocument
```

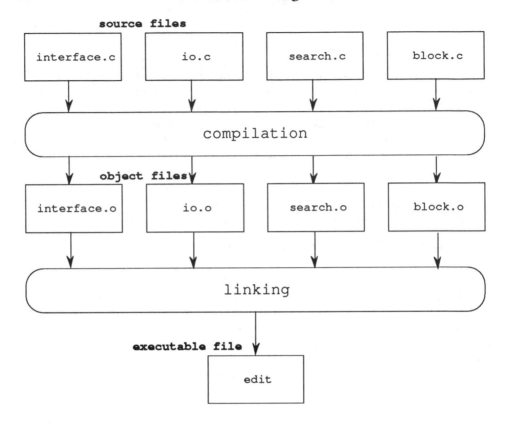

10.2 Declarations and Definitions

We need to be clear about the difference between the declaration and definition of identifiers

identifier   the name of a variable or a function
declaration   a specification of how an identifier is to be used
definition   a declaration which also reserves space for a variable or sets out the body of a function
prototype   a declaration of a function

Some examples in which the identifier `thing` is used to express different quantities, may help :

```
declaration of variables:
int    thing;                     /* int */
float  thing;                     /* float */
char   *thing;                    /* pointer to char */
double thing[];                   /* array of double */
short  *thing[];                  /* array of pointers to short */
long   (*thing)(char, int);       /* pointer to a function taking a
                                     char and an int argument,
                                     returning a long */
```

```
declaration of functions:
int     thing(float, char *);        /* function taking float and char*
                                        arguments, returning int */
float   *thing(void);                /* function taking no arguments,
                                        returning pointer to float */
int     thing();                     /* function returning int,
                                        arguments unspecified */
```

An identifier may be declared more than once at one level of the program but each declaration must be the same. Inside a compound statement, the identifier may be re-declared to have a different meaning; this will hide the meaning which exists outside the compound statement.

10.3   Internal and External Identfiers

Variables may be declared to be internal to a function, or more particularly, internal to a compound statement, or external to all functions. Functions can only be declared to be external to all other functions.

For an external variable or function its defintion and declaration may coincide or it may have one definition and multiple declarations; however, all declarations of the same identifier must be identical. It is good practice to provide a declaration of each function, in the form of a prototype, near the top of each source file. The declaration of a variable differs from its definition in that the keyword extern is used; for functions, the use of extern is optional:

```
int     thing;                       /* variable definition */
extern int     thing;                /* variable declaration */
extern char    *string;              /* variable declaration */
extern float  function(void);        /* function declaration */
float   function(void);              /* function declaration */
```

For an internal variable its definition and declaration always coincide. For all variables there must be a declaration before the first use of a variable.

10.3.1 Scope of Identifiers

The scope of an identifier is the range of statements within which it can be used:

internal identifier	from its point of declaration to the end of the compound statement in which it is declared
external identifier	from its point of declaration to the end of the file in which it is declared
formal argument to function	from its point of declaration to the end of the compound statement which forms the body of the function

Program Extract 10.1

```
int     extVar1;              /* definition and declaration */
extern float  extVar2;        /* declaration */

char    *func1(int);          /* declaration i.e. prototype */

char *func1(int param1)       /* function and parameter
                                 definition */
{
   long   local1 = 2 * param; /* definition */

   ...
   /* can access extVar1, extVar2, func1, param1 and local1 */
   ...
}

float   extVar2;              /* definition */
long    extVar3;              /* definition */

int func2(long param2)
{
   char    local2;
   int     local3;
   double param2;             /* hides long parameter:
                                 very bad practice */

   ...
   /* can access extVar1, extVar2, extVar3, func1, func2,
          param2(double version), local2 and local3 */
   ...
   {                          /* inner compound statement */
      long    extVar1;        /* hides int version */
      float  local2;          /* hides char version */
      double local4;

      ...
      /* can access extVar1 (long version), extVar2, extVar3, func1,
         func2, param2(double version), local2 (float version)
         and local4 */
      ...
   }
   ...
   /* can access extVar1(int version), extVar2, extVar3, func1,
        func2, param2(double version), local2(char version)
           and local3 */
   ...
}
```

In Program Extract 10.1 the external, or global, variable ext Var1 can be accessed from within each of the functions, except from within the inner compound statement in func2() which redefines it as a long variable. On the other hand extVar2 can be accessed from any part of either function. Although it has not been defined until after func1() it has nevertheless been declared before func1()

and is thus accessible everywhere after its declaration; this approach of splitting the declaration and definition is unusual and is only here for illustration.

The variable `extVar3` in only accessible from within `func2()` since its declaration does not appear until after `func1()`. `func1()` shows how its parameter, `param1`, can be used to initialise an internal variable, `local`, which are both only accessible from within the body of that function.

`func2()` illustrates a problem that sometimes occurs by mistake: the parameter, `param2`, has been redefined as an internal variable which hides the use of the parameter. This is not something that you would do intentionally but it is necessary to be aware of the possibility in readiness for the time when you misspell an identifier. This function also contains an example of an internal variable, `local2`, being hidden by another of the same name in the inner compound statement. It should be noted that after this inner compound statement the variables, `extVar1` and `local2`, which are now visible again, still contain the values they had before this compound statement was entered.

10.4   Static Variables and Functions

The `static` storage class provides two useful but different facilities:

i)   it provides permanent storage for internal variables

ii)   it allows us to restrict the scope of external identifiers representing either variables or functions to the file in which they are defined.

The first use was discussed in Section 8.1.3. Here, we will pay attention to the second use. It is unfortunate that the one keyword has two distinctly different meanings.

To provide static storage for any variable or function, it is necessary to precede the defintion and all declarations of its identifier by the keyword `static`:

```
static int    thing;
static void   func(int);
```

10.5   Storage Allocation

We discussed some aspects of storage allocation in Chapter 8, paying particular attention to the use of the libarary function `malloc()` and its related functions. Apart from this means of dynamic storage allocation, under the control of the programmer, storage for variables is allocated in two different ways by the system; either prior to the start of program execution or automatically during the course of execution:

i)   for *external variables* and *internal static variables:* before the start of program execution; this storage is not released until the end of program execution

ii)   for *internal automatic variables:* at their point of definition; this storage is released at the end of the enclosing compound statement

iii)   for the *formal parameters to functions*: on entry to the function; this storage is
        released upon exit from the function

The section of storage used for i) is sometimes called *the heap* and that for ii) and
iii) is sometimes called *the stack*.

10.6 Initialisation

A variable can only be initialised when it is defined since this is the time when
storage is allocated. The method of allocating storage determines what type of
initialisation is possible and what can be assumed about uninitialised variables.

Any variable allocated on the heap, i.e. external variables and internal static
variables can only be initialised with constant values. Any variable allocated on the
stack, i.e. internal automatic variables and function parameters, can be initialised
with any meaningful expression. There is however one exception. Aggregates, in
the form of arrays and structures, can only be initialised with constants regardless of
whether they are internal or external.

If a variable is not explicitly initialised its contents depend of whether its storage is
in the heap or on the stack. If in the heap, it is guaranteed to contain the value
zero. If on the stack, its contents cannot be relied upon; put another way, it is
guaranteed to contain garbage!

10.7 Summary

We will illustrate this collection of points by some elements of a multi-file
program. The source is distributed over three files, suitably named `file1.c`,
`file2.c` and `file3.c`. The types of the variables and functions have no
significance in the context of this discussion and have been set arbitrarily.

We will discuss which identifiers are accessible from each of the files.

File 1

```
/* variable definitions */
int    extVar1;                    /* zero by default */
int    extVar2 = 7;

static long   extVar3;             /* zero by default */
static float  extVar4 = 3.5;

int    extVar5[] = {3, 5, 9};      /* an array of size 3 */

int    extVar6[5] = {1, 6};        /* remaining elements are
                                      zero */

/* function prototypes */
float func1(int);                  /* definition in this file */
void  func3(char);                 /* definition in file 2 */
long  func5(char *);               /* definition in file 3 */


static void func2(void);           /* private to this file */

main()
{
}

float func1(int param1)
{
   char   localVar1;               /* contains garbage */
   int    localVar2 = 7;

   static int    localVar3;
   static int    localVar4 = 3;

   int    localVar5 = param1 * param1;

}

static void func2()
{
   long   localVar6;
   static unsigned  localVar7;

}
```

end of file 1

File 2

```
/* variable declarations */
extern int    extVar2;
extern int    extVar5[];
extern int    extVar6[];

/* variable definitions */
int    extVar3;                    /* re-use variable for this
                                      file */

static long    extVar7;

/* function prototypes */
float func1(int);                  /* definition in file 1 */
void  func3(char);                 /* definition in this file */
long  func5(char *);               /* definition in file 3 */

static long    func4(void);        /* private to this file */


void func3(char param2)
{
}

static long func4()
{
}
```

end of file 2

File 3

```
/* variable declarations */
extern int    extVar1;
extern int    extVar2;
extern int    extVar5[];
extern int    extVar6[];

extern int    extVar3;             /* to access the definition
                                      in file2 */

/* variable definition */
static double extVar8;             /* private to this file */
```

```
/* function prototypes */
float  func1(int);                    /* definition in file 1 */
void   func3(char);                   /* definition in file 2 */
long   func5(char *);                 /* definition in this file */

static int     *func6(void);          /* private to this file */

long func5(char *param3)
{
}

static int *func6()
{
}
```

end of file 3

We will take a number of different views of this multi-file program. In particular we will note, from the point of view of the functions in each file, which variables and functions are accessible and which are inaccessible.

The View From `file 1`
The functions in file 1 can access:

variables defined in file	extVar1, extVar2, extVar3, extVar4, extVar5, extVar6
functions defined in file 1	func1(), func2()
function defined in file 2	func3()
function defined in file 3	func5()

The functions cannot access:

variables defined in file 2	extVar3, extVar7
function defined in file 2	func4()
variable defined in file 3	extVar8
function defined in file 3	func6()

The variables `extVar3` and `extVar4` and the function `func2()` are only accessible from within this file since they have been declared to be `static`. Note that this definition of `extVar3` hides from view another definition of the same identifier in file 2.

The variables `extVar2` and `extVar4` are initialised with constant values; `extVar1` and `extVar3` are initialised to zero. For the array variable `extVar5`, its size is determined by the number of initialisers. The array `extVar6` has five elements the first two of which are initialised to the given constants and the remaining three elements are set to zero.

Within the function `func1()`, the variable `localVar1` is uninitialised and thus we cannot assume that it contains any particular value; on the other hand `localVar2` is intialised to the value 7. The `static` variables `localVar3` and `localVar4` are initialised prior to the first entry to the function, the first, by default, to zero and the other to 3. If the value of either variable is altered within the function, that value is preserved for the next entry to this function. The variables are *not re-initialised*. Conversely, the local automatic variables, `localVar1`, `localVar2` and `localVar5`, are created each and every time the function is entered and thus are always initialised upon entry. More precisely, the initial value of `localVar1` is unreliable, that of `localVar2` is always 7 and that of `localVar5` is dependent on the value of `param1`.

The View From `file 2`
The functions in file 2 can access:

variables defined in file 1	extVar2, extVar5, extVar6
function defined in file 1	func1()
variables defined in file 2	extVar3, extVar7
functions defined in file 2	func3(), func4()
function defined in file 3	func5()

The functions cannot access:

variable defined in file 1	extVar1, extVar3, extVar4
function defined in file 1	func2()
variable defined in file 3	extVar8
function defined in file 3	func6()

The external variable extVar1 which is defined in file 1 is potentially accessible within file 2 but because there is no declaration in file 2 it cannot, at present, be used. The variable extVar3, in file 1, was declared to be static and thus private to file 1; we can thus re-use its name in this file to represent another quantity.

This file also sets up its own private quantities extVar7 and func4().

The View From `file 3`
The functions in file 3 can access:

variables defined in file 1	extVar1, extVar2, extVar5, extVar6
functions defined in file 1	func1()
variable defined in file 2	extVar3
function defined in file 2	func3()
variable defined in file 3	extVar8
functions defined in file 3	func5(), func6()

The functions cannot access:

variable defined in file 1	extVar3, extVar4
function defined in file 1	func2()
variable defined in file 2	extVar7
function defined in file 2	func4()

Managing the many possibilities that these rules make available can be a problem. It is good practice to define, and possibly initialise, all external, global variables in just one file. For ease of maintenance this file need not contain any functions.

For each source file, place the function prototypes for the functions defined in that file in a suitably named header file and then include that header file in every other file that needs to use any of these functions. The definitions of any external static variables and prototypes of any static functions can safely be placed in the source file itself, instead of in the header file, since these cannot be used by functions in other files.

The View From The Variables

We can also set out in tabular form, where each variable has been defined and from which files it is accessible. For example, `extVar2` has been defined and initialised in `file1` and has been declared, and thus made accessible, in `file2` and `file3`.

	file1	file2	file3
extVar1	defined zeroed	potentially accessible but not declared	declared
extVar2	defined initialised	declared	declared
extVar3	defined zeroed	inaccessible	inaccessible
extVar3	inaccessible	defined zeroed	declared
extVar4	defined initialised	inaccessible	inaccessible
extVar5	defined initialised	declared	declared
extVar6	defined initialised	declared	declared
extVar7	inaccessible	defined zeroed	inaccessible
extVar8	incaccessible	inaccessible	defined zeroed

The View From The Functions

The final view sets out where each function has been defined and from which files it is accessible. For example, func1() has been defined in file1 and is accessible from file2 and file3; whereas func2() has been declared to be static in file1 and is thus inaccessible from file2 and file3.

	file1	file2	file3
func1()	defined	declared	declared
func2()	defined	inaccessible	inaccessible
func3()	declared	defined	declared
func4()	inaccessible	defined	inaccessible
func5()	declared	declared	defined
func6()	inaccessible	inaccessible	defined

11

The Pre-Processor

The language provides a pre-processor which, as its name indicates, carries out certain actions on the source file before it is presented to the compiler. These actions consist of:

- replacement of defined identifiers by pieces of text (#define)

- conditional selection of parts of a source file (#ifdef ...)

- inclusion of other source files (#include)

11.1 Pre-processor Directives

When a source file is presented to the compiler, it is automatically passed through a pre-processor which can carry out a number of text manipulation operations. The modified source is then considered by the compiler itself. Compilers usually provide some means of examining the source file immediately after the pre-processing although you should not need to do this very often.

Each instruction to the pre-processor is known as a *directive* which must occupy a line of its own and begin with one of the following:

```
#define
#include
#ifdef
#ifndef
#else
#elif
#endif
#undef
```

There are a small number of others which have specialised use and are not covered here.

11.2 Macro Definition

We have already seen how we can give names to constants which are to be used in places such as the dimension of an array.

```
#define   arraySize 250

int    anArray[arraySize];
```

When the source file is presented to the pre-processor, every occurrence of the identifier `arraySize` is replaced by the constant `250`. Whether this is meaningful or not is determined by the compiler when it considers the file after pre-processing. Note that there is no semi-colon at the end of the `#define` line. If there were, the array declaration, after pre-processing, would be like:

```
#define   arraySize 250;

int    anArray[arraySize];

/* after pre-processing: */
int    anArray[250;];                          /* syntax error */
```

Some compilers, in drawing attention to this error, show the faulty line after pre-processing but, unfortunately, some display the original line or simply refer to the original file by line number. It can then be difficult to appreciate what has gone wrong and that the cause of the problem is at a different place in the source file, namely in the macro definition.

The pre-processor is not concerned with the presence or absence of a semi-colon; it simply replaces every occurrence of the identifier, `arraySize`, by the remainder of the line. The general form is thus:

#define   *identifier   replacement_text*

Whether the replacement text makes any sense is not the concern of the pre-processor but of the compiler itself. Possibilities include:

```
#define   CTRLZ     '\032'                   /* control-Z */
#define   clear     putchar(CTRLZ)           /* clear the screen */
#define   newline   putchar('\n')
#define   forever   for(;;)
#define   begin     {                        /* for Pascal programmers */
```

Returning, for the moment, to the question of the inclusion of a semi-colon. Consider what would happen if we had defined `newline` to be:

```
#define   newline   putchar('\n');

if(clearScreen)  clear;
else             newline;
```

This would create no problem since the file, after pre-processing, would appear as:

```
if(clearScreen)  putchar('\032');
else              putchar('\n');;      /* note the double semi-colon */
```

Although an extra semi-colon has appeared, it creates no problem. Consider, however, what would happen if we were to make a simple change:

```
if(!clearScreen) newline;
else             clear;
```

which, after pre-processing, would become:

```
if(!clearScreen) putchar('\n');;      /* note the double semi-colon */
else             putchar('\032');                  /* syntax error */
```

Now we can see that the extra semi-colon does cause an error by detaching the `else` from its corresponding `if`. We could, of course, remember that `newline` carries with it its own semi-colon but the code looks more natural the way it is written.

In summary, it is unwise to place a semi-colon at the end of the pre-processor line.

11.3   Macros With Arguments

A macro may have arguments in which case its use has the appearance of a function call. There is however no overhead of a function call which may be an advantage but there can be problems which need to be handled with care. The general form is:

> **#define**   *identifier(arg1, arg2, ...) replacement_text*

Note that there must be no space between *identifier* and *(*. If there were, the line would be regarded as a simple `#define` macro with the parentheses and arguments being part of the replacement text.

Every occurrence of each argument, `arg1, arg2` ... is replaced by the corresponding actual argument when the macro is used. Consider the question of finding the maximum of two given values:

```
#define   max(a, b) a>b? a : b

main()
{
    int    thisInt, thatInt, result;
    float  thisFloat, thatFloat, answer;

            /* calculation to give values to variables */

    result = max(thisInt, thatInt);
    answer = max(thisFloat, thatFloat);

    result = max(thisInt++, thatInt);
    result = max(thisInt + thatInt, 240);

}
```

which, after pre-processing, becomes:

```
main()
{
    int    thisInt, thatInt, result;
    float  thisFloat, thatFloat, answer;

               /* calculation to give values to variables */

    result = thisInt> thatInt? thisInt :  thatInt;
    answer = thisFloat> thatFloat? thisFloat :  thatFloat;

    result = thisInt++> thatInt? thisInt++ :  thatInt;
    result = thisInt + thatInt> 240? thisInt + thatInt :  240;

}
```

From this we can see an advantage and a disadvantage of using a macro in place of a function. Since a macro is only concerned with textual replacement it has no knowledge of the C types. This means that its arguments can be of any type. In this example we have found the maximum of two integers and then of two floats.

If however the actual arguments are not simple quantities, problems can arise. Where an actual argument is to be incremented we see that two incrementations may take place. Where an expression, here in the form of an addition, is to be carried out, a syntax error can occur. Fortunately the second problem can be overcome is we are careful when we define the macro and make judicious use of parentheses. The first problem, concerned with incrementation, cannot be overcome.

The preferred way of writing the macro is:

```
#define    max(a, b)  (((a)>(b))? (a) : (b))
```

which would produce the following code after pre-processing:

```
main()
{
    int    thisInt, thatInt, result;
    float  thisFloat, thatFloat, answer;

    result = (((thisInt)>( thatInt))? (thisInt) : ( thatInt));
    answer = (((thisFloat)>( thatFloat))? (thisFloat) : ( thatFloat));

    result = (((thisInt++)>( thatInt))? (thisInt++) : ( thatInt));
    result = (((thisInt + thatInt)>( 240))? (thisInt + thatInt) : ( 240
}
```

Although this seems overburdened with parentheses, it is at least syntactically correct. Remember that we rarely need to examine the file after the pre-processor stage.

11.3.1 Arguments Within Strings

One use of macros with arguments is to provide a simple way of outputting the names and associated values of variables when debugging a program. Since a macro can handle variables of different types, it would be appropriate to provide a format specifier in order to control the layout. A typical use would be:

```
main()
{
   int    thing  = 29;
   float  object = 13.5;

   /*  some calculations to alter thing and object */

   debug(thing, d);                    /* print as decimal */
   debug(thing, x);                    /* print as hexadecimal */
   debug(object, f);                   /* print as float */
   /* ... */
}
```

with intended output being:

```
thing = 29
thing = 1d
object = 13.5
```

Our first attempt at the macro, debug, might be:

```
#define   debug(var, format)   printf("var = %format\n", var)
```

Unfortunately, this produces the following, distinctly unhelpful output:

```
var = 0.000000ormat
var = 0.000000ormat
var = 13.500000ormat
```

If we examine the file immediately after the pre-processor, we find:

```
      printf("var = %format\n", thing);
      printf("var = %format\n", thing);
      printf("var = %format\n", object);
```

The identifier var has been correctly replaced by thing and by object outside the quotation marks but not within them; and, similarly, the identifier format has not been replaced. To overcome this problem, a special device is offered. In the replacement text of the macro definition:

a)   if an identifier is immediately preceded by #, its associated replacement is enclosed in quotation marks

b)   and, consecutive string constants are concatenated into one string

We thus write the macro in the form:

```
#define   debug(var, format)   printf(#var " = %" #format "\n", var)
```

which after the pre-processor produces:

```
      printf("thing" " = %" "d" "\n", thing);
      printf("thing" " = %" "x" "\n", thing);
      printf("object" " = %" "f" "\n", object);
```

and the desired final output of:

```
thing = 29
thing = 1d
object = 13.5
```

Progam 4.1 in chapter 4 contained many `printf()` statements in order to display the size of each of the basic types. When we use a new computer, we frequently run Program 11.1 to fulfill the same purpose.

Program 11.1
_____

```
#include <stdio.h>

#define size(type)  printf("Size of " #type ": %d\n", sizeof(type))

main()
{
    size(char);
    size(signed char);
    size(unsigned char);
    size(short);
    size(int);
    size(unsigned);
    size(long);
    size(unsigned long);
    size(float);
    size(double);
}
```

Sample output (on a Macintosh IIci)
_____

```
Size of char: 1
Size of signed char: 1
Size of unsigned char: 1
Size of short: 2
Size of int: 4
Size of unsigned: 4
Size of long: 4
Size of unsigned long: 4
Size of float: 4
Size of double: 8
```
_____

It is left as an exercise to modify this so that the numbers are aligned.

11.4   Conditional Selection

The pre-processor enables you to select conditionally parts of any source file for onward presentation to the compiler. Normally all the source code is passed to the compiler but it is possible to arrange matters so that groups of lines are only passed if some condition holds; and conversely, if some condition does not hold.

The directives available for this are:

```
#ifdef    identifier              /* if identifier is defined */
#ifndef   identifier              /* if identifier is not defined */
#else
#endif
```

There are many potential uses but will illustrate two commonly found situations: when we wish to produce a program which will be compiled on different versions of the compiler or on different types of hardware; and when we wish to incorporate into the source file some debugging or testing code. Each of these requires some lines of code to be specific to one particular set of circumstances.

11.4.1 Portability

To maintain many versions of one program each of which differs from the others in only a minor way can give rise to enormous problems.

Pre-standard compilers did not support function prototypes although functions declarations which indicate the return type of the function without specifying the number and types of the arguments were supported. It would be cumbersome to maintain two copies of a program, one with prototypes and the other with old fashioned function declarations. Fortunately, compilers that purport to conform to the ANSI Standard define the name __STD__ (the name begins and end with two underscore characters). To make a program portable across these different compilers, conditional selection would be used:

```
#ifdef __STDC__
                                /* function prototypes */
void    func1(char *, float);
char    *func2(const int *, long);
#else
                                /* function declarations */
void    func1();
char    *func2();
#endif
```

The source code passed onto the compiler by the pre-processor would contain either the prototypes or the declarations but not both.

Another example is where different suppliers of compilers may require you to include different header files to handle situations not covered by the Standard, for example:

```
#ifdef __TURBO__
                                /* Borland turbo C */
  #include <io.h>
  #include <dir.h>
#else
#ifdef __ZTC__
                                /* Zortech C */
  #include <dos.h>
#endif
```

Conditional inclusion can be used anywhere is a file. Suppose that a function, fileName(), needs to extract a file name from a full pathname that has been provided as its argument. Different operating systems have different conventions for full pathnames:

```
/home/programs/project/prog.c        /* Unix pathname */
c:\home\programs\project\prog.c       /* MSDOS pathname */
home:programs:project:prog.c          /* Macintosh */
```

In each case, we wish to extract prog.c . The function would need to search the given string for the rightmost '/' on Unix, '\' on MSDOS and ':' on Macintosh. Furthermore, on MSDOS, if the string contains no '\', the ':' must be sought.

Program 11.2

```
#include <stdio.h>
#include <stdlib.h>
#include <string.h>

char    *fileName(char *pathname);

main()
{
    char    path[BUFSIZ];    /* BUFSIZ is a pre-defined large value */
    char    *system;                    /* to point to system name */

#ifdef MAC
    printf("testing for the Macintosh\n");
    system = "Macintosh";
#endif
#ifdef MSDOS
    printf("testing for MSDOS\n");
    system = "MS-DOS";
#endif
#ifdef UNIX
    printf("testing for Unix\n");
    system = "Unix";
#endif
    while( printf("Enter %s path: ", system),gets(path) != NULL)
        printf("file name: [%s]\n", fileName(path));
}

char    *fileName(char *pathname)
{
    char    *separator;
    char    *name;          /* a pointer to the string to be returned */

#ifdef MAC
    separator = strrchr(pathname, ':');
#else
 #ifdef UNIX
    separator = strrchr(pathname, '/');
 #else
  #ifdef MSDOS
```

```
        separator = strrchr(pathname, '\\');
        if(separator == NULL)
            separator = strrchr(pathname, ':');
  #endif
 #endif
#endif
    if(separator == NULL)
        separator = pathname;                    /* simple file name */
    else
        separator++;          /* file name is to right of separator */

                                      /* allocate sufficient space */
    name = (char *)malloc(strlen(separator + 1));
    if(name == NULL)
    {
        printf("out of storage\n");
        exit(1);
    }

    strcpy(name, separator);          /* copy into allocated space */
    return name;
}
```

Program 11.2   (after pre-processing with MSDOS defined)

```
/* Note that only those pieces of code relevant to this system have
   been included. */

char    *fileName(char *pathname);

main()
{
    char    path[1024 ];
    char    *system;

    printf("testing for MSDOS\n");
    system = "MS-DOS";

    while( printf("Enter %s path: ", system),gets(path) != 0)
        printf("file name: [%s]\n", fileName(path));
}

char    *fileName(char *pathname)
{
    char    *separator;
    char    *name;     /* a pointer to the string to be returned */

    separator = strrchr(pathname, '\\');
    if(separator == 0)
        separator = strrchr(pathname, ':');

    if(separator == 0)
        separator = pathname;          /* simple file name */
    else
```

```
        separator++; /* file name is to right of separator */

                        /* allocate sufficient space */
    name = (char *)malloc(strlen(separator + 1));
    if(name == 0)
    {
        printf("out of storage\n");
        exit(1);
    }

    strcpy(name, separator);   /* copy into allocated space */
    return name;
}
```

Sample input(in bold) and output

```
testing for MSDOS
Enter MS-DOS path: c:\home\programs\project\prog.c
file name: [prog.c]
Enter MS-DOS path: c:prog.c
file name: [prog.c]
Enter MS-DOS path: prog.c
file name: [prog.c]
Enter MS-DOS path: ..\project\prog.c
file name: [prog.c]
```

It must be admitted that the source code is now more difficult to read even though it can be used on the three different systems. On the other hand, it focuses attention on those parts of the code which need to be different on each system and which are the same. For illustration, in the main() function we have used three separate #ifdef sections whereas in the fileName() function these have been nested.

We have used names such as MAC, MSDOS and UNIX which are not pre-defined. We therefore need to define the appropriate one for the system in use at any time. One way to do this is to edit the source file and place at the top of the file the appropriate definition:

```
#define    UNIX
```

Another is to use a facility available with most compilers which allows us to specify names which are to be defined for this compilation. For example, on a Unix system a -D flag may be followed by an identifier which we wish to define and has the same effect as the above approach; the compilation could then be:

```
cc -DUNIX -o filename filename.c
```

11.4.2 Test Code

Suppose that we wish to write a function compile() to create and issue the command to compile a given file. The standard library contains a function system() which issues its argument, as a string, to the operating system. The compile() function needs to assemble the string and then use system().

We want our function ultimately to be used as an object file which could become part of a library. However, we need to create, for testing purposes, an executable file with its own main() function simply to ensure that our function will work. It would be useful to keep this main() function with the compile() function so that the latter always has some testing facility in its source code. In addition to this, during this testing phase, it may be unwise to issue a command by means of system() because we may get things wrong. It would be wiser simply to print out the command we would issue:

Program 11.3

```
#include <stdio.h>
#include <stdlib.h>
#include <string.h>

#define maxSize   256

void    compile(char * source);

void compile(char *source)
{
    char    command[maxSize];
    char    object[maxSize];

    strcpy(object, source);
    *strrchr(object, '.') = '\0';                    /* strip the .c */

    sprintf(command, "cc -o %s %s", object, source);
#ifndef TEST
    system(command);                                 /* issue the command */
#else
    printf("Command issued: [%s]\n", command);
#endif
}

#ifdef TEST
main()
{
    compile("something.c");
}
#endif
```

On a Unix system this can be compiled for test purposes by:

```
cc -DTEST -o compile compile.c
```

where the output would be:

```
Command issued: [cc -o something something.c]
```

and when we are satisfied that this works correctly, we can create the object file by:

```
cc -c compile.c
```

11.5   Inclusion of Files

The directive to include the contents of other files comes in two forms:

```
#include   <filename>
#include   "filename"
```

Each causes the entire contents of the named file to replace this occurrence of the directive. The only difference between them is where in the file system the pre-processor looks for the file. In the first version, the file to be included is assumed to be in a standard place in the file system. In the second version, the directory containing the source file is searched and then, if the file is not found, the standard place is searched. The location of this standard place is the concern of the operating system and is not defined in the language.

The commonly used header files such as those needed by the standard library e.g. stdio.h, stdlib.h, math.h ... are put in the standard place. Header files specific to a particular program are most likely placed in the same directory as the source files. We would typically write:

```
#include   <stdio.h>
#include   <stlib.h>
#include   <math.h>
#include   <ctype.h>

#include   "myHeader.h"
```

We considered the structure of multi-file programs in Chapter 10. We can now extend this discussion to consider how to manage the declarations, prototypes and variable defintions. A common practice is to have, for each source file, an associated header file of the same base name but with the suffix .h in place of .c . For a source file edit.c we would have a header file edit.h . In this header file we place the prototypes of the publicly available functions; that is, those which have not been defined to be static. The declarations of all the external variables can be placed in one file, globals.h, so that each of the other header files can include it.

We need to guard against one possible problem: a file must not be included more than once. The standard way to overcome this problem is to select the complete contents of the file conditionally:

```
#ifndef   myHeader_h
#define   myHeader_h

/* contents of the header file called myHeader.h */

#endif
```

An identifier, similar to the name of the file is constructed. Since, however, a period (.) is not a legal character within an identifier, it is replaced by the underscore (_) . When this file is first included, the identifier myHeader_h is undefined. It is then immediately defined, although not to any particular value and the contents of the file are included. Any subsequent attempt to include this file will discover that the myHeader_h is now defined and the inclusion will not be repeated. To minimise the danger of this identifier coinciding with another of the same name within the file, a common practice is to surround it with underscores: _myHeader_h_ .

The multi-file program would look like:

```
file: globals.h
#ifndef   _globals_h_
#define   _globals_h_
extern int    thisOne;
extern float  thatOne;
...
#endif
```

```
file: file1.h
#ifndef   _file1_h_
#define   _file1_h_

#include  "globals"
#include  <stdio.h>
#include  <stdlib.h>

/* function prototypes */
void   func1(int, char);
char   *func2(char *);
...
#endif
```

```
file: file1.c
#include  "file1.h"  /* prototypes for the functions in this file */
#include  "file2.h"  /* need prototypes for functions in file2.c */
#include  "file3.h"  /* need prototypes for functions in file3.c */

/* definitions of static external variables */
static int    something;
static char   days[] = {31,28,31,30,31,30,31,31,30,31,30,31};

/* prototypes of static functions
static int    function1(void);
static void   function2(char **);

/* function definitions */

void   func1(int anInt, char aChar)
{
    /* body of function */
}

char   *func2(char * message)
{
    /* body of function */
}
```

A similar arrangement needs to be made for each of `file2.c`, `file2.h`, `file3.c`, `file3.h` ...

The final consideration is the *definition* of the global variables. If any need to be initialised then the following approach is possible. The `main()` function can be placed in any of the source files but a feasible place is here:

```
file: globals.c
#include   "globals.h"

int    thisOne = 5;
float  thatOne = 1.2;
. . .

main()
{
       /* body of function */
}
```

If no variable needs to be initialised, the following approach can be adopted:

```
file: globals.c
#define     extern
#include    "globals.h"

main()
{
       /* body of function */
}
```

The `#define` states that the identifier `extern` is to replaced by nothing. Since this deliberately precedes the inclusion of `globals.h`, every entry in that file has the identifier `extern` stripped off, making each declaration into a definition.

12

Input and Output

Any useful program needs to be able to communicate with its environment by reading from the keyboard or a file and writing to the screen or a file. The language itself has no input and output statements but the Standard has defined a library of useful functions. We shall summarise, in the next chapter, the contents of the library but will pay particular attention, in this chapter, to those that support input and output.

Before any transfer of data can take place between the program and any external file or device, a link has to be set up by means of *opening a file*. This establishes a *stream* via which the program can communicate with its environment. For each open stream, a structure of type FILE, defined in the header file stdio.h, is created. This contains information needed to control a stream, including its file position indicator, a pointer to its associated buffer, an error indicator and an end of file indicator. A stream uses a pointer to this structure and is therefore a variable of type FILE *.

Before using any function which handles input or output, it is necessary to include the header file:

```
#include  <stdio.h>
```

12.1 Standard Streams

Before the start of program execution, three standard streams are automatically created for you:

```
FILE    *stdin;                      /* standard input */
FILE    *stdout;                     /* standard output */
FILE    *stderr;                     /* standard error output */
```

What these streams are connected to is a matter for the operating system. Typically stdin is connected to the keyboard and stdout and stderr to the terminal screen. However by means of re-direction, many operating system provide a means of connecting these to files without affecting the contents of the program.

Some functions in the library, such as `printf()` and `getchar()`, support input and output only via these standard streams and others permit the use of any stream.

12.2   Opening and Closing Files

If we wish to open a stream, other than the standard ones, we need to use the function:

```
FILE    *fopen(const char *fileName, const char *mode);
```

where `fileName` is a character string containing the external name of the file and `mode` is one of the following:

r   open an existing file for reading

w   open a file for writing; if the file exists, its length is trucated to zero; if it does not exist, it is created

a   open a file for writing; if the file exists, subsequent writes are placed at the end; if it does not exist, it is created

If the file needs to be opened for both reading and writing, the modes become `'r+'`, `'w+'` and `'a+'`.

Two types of stream are supported: *text streams* and *binary streams*. The first consists of lines of characters such that output is intelligible to the human eye; the second is simply a sequence of bytes and is only intelligible to programs. The functions to be used for text streams include `printf()`, `getchar()`, `putchar()` ... ; functions for binary streams include `fread()`, `fwrite()`, `ftell()` .... For binary streams, the mode needs to include the letter `'b'` such as `"rb"`, `"r+b"` or `"rb+"`.

Attempting to open, for reading, a non-existent file, or one for which you do not have the appropriate permission causes an error. If `fopen()` is unable to open a file successfully it returns the value `NULL`. When it is successful, the function returns a pointer which needs to be assigned to a variable for later use:

```
#include   <stdio.h>

FILE    *input;
FILE    *output;

input = fopen("unsorted.data", "r");
if(input == NULL)
    printf("unable to open file for reading\n");

if((output = fopen("sorted.date", "w")) == NULL)
    printf("unable to open file for writing\n");
```

When all transfers to or from a file have been completed it is necessary to close it by:

```
int    fclose(FILE    *stream);
```

If any error occurs when attempting to close a file, `fclose()` returns EOF, otherwise it returns zero. The two files, opened above, would be closed by:

```
fclose(input);
fclose(output);
```

Program 12.1

```
#include  <stdio.h>
#include  <stdlib.h>

main(int argc, char *argv[])
{
    FILE    *inputFile;
    FILE    *outputFile;
    int     aChar;

    if(argc < 3)
    {
        fprintf(stderr, "insufficient arguments\n");
        exit(1);
    }

    if((inputFile = fopen(argv[1], "r")) == NULL)
    {
        fprintf(stderr, "cannot open %s\n", argv[1]);
        exit(2);
    }

    if((outputFile = fopen(argv[2], "w")) == NULL)
    {
        fprintf(stderr, "cannot open %s for writing\n", argv[2]);
        exit(3);
    }
                                    /* everthing seems to be OK */
    while((aChar = getc(inputFile)) != EOF)
        putc(aChar, outputFile);

    exit(0);
}
```

12.3 Transferring Single Characters

Functions for reading individual characters are:

```
int     getchar(void);
int     getc(FILE *stream);
int     fgetc(FILE *stream);
```

`fgetc()` gets and returns the next character from the input `stream`; if the stream is at the end of file, EOF is returned. `getc()` is equivalent but may be implemented as a macro; for this reason, its argument should never be an expression with side effects. `getchar()` is a special form of `getc()` which only reads from `stdin`.

Similar functions are available for writing individual characters:

```
int     putchar(int aChar);
int     putc(int aChar, FILE *stream);
int     fputc(int aChar, FILE *stream);
```

`fputc()` writes `aChar` to the given output `stream`; `putc()` is equivalent and may be a macro; `putchar()` only writes to `stdout`. Each function returns the character written unless an error has occurred, in which case it returns `EOF`.

Program 12.1 expects to be provided with two arguments which are the names of files. It then copies the contents of the first file to the second.

12.3.1 Re-reading a Character

In Chapter 3, we wrote a program to find the length of the longest word in the input stream. This needed a function to skip the space between consecutive words and another to read and count the characters in a word. Each function only knew that its work was complete when it had read one character too many. This was then put back onto the input stream by the `ungetc()` function:

```
int     ungetc(int aChar, FILE *stream);
```

The function to find the length of a word is repeated here:

```
int wordLength(void)
{
    int aChar;
    int length = 0;

    aChar=getchar();
    while(isalnum(aChar))         /* is it acceptable? */
    {
        length++;                 /* increase the length count */
        aChar=getchar();
    }
    ungetc(aChar, stdin);         /* put back extra character */
    return length;
}
```

12.4 Transferring Character Strings

Functions for reading complete character strings are:

```
char    *gets(char *string);
char    *fgets(char *string, int n, FILE *stream);
```

The parameter `string` is assumed to point to an array of characters. `gets()` reads characters from `stdin`, placing them in this array. It continues to read until it

Program 12.2

```
#include   <stdio.h>
#include   <stdlib.h>
#include   <string.h>

#define    stringLength 20
#define    nameSize      200

main()
{
    FILE   *inputFile;
    FILE   *outputFile;
    char   fileName[nameSize];
    char   string[stringLength];

    puts("Source file: ");
    gets(fileName);
    if(strlen(fileName) == 0)
    {
        puts("Using standard input stream");
        inputFile = stdin;
    }
    else if((inputFile = fopen(fileName, "r")) == NULL)
    {
        fprintf(stderr, "cannot open [%s]\n", fileName);
        exit(2);
    }

    fputs("Destination file: ", stdout);
    if((outputFile = fopen(gets(fileName), "w")) == NULL)
    {
        fprintf(stderr, "cannot open [%s] for writing\n", fileName);
        exit(3);
    }
                                /* everthing seems to be OK */
    while((fgets(string, stringLength, inputFile)) != NULL)
        fputs(string, outputFile);

    exit(0);
}
```

Sample dialogue (input in bold):

```
Source file:
xxx.⏎
Destination file: zzz
```

```
Source file:
⏎
Using standard input stream
Destination file: xxx
```

encounters a new-line character or the end of file. The new-line character is not stored but a null character is placed in the array. The function returns a pointer to the first character of the array, if it was successful; if no characters were read or end of file was encountered, it returns NULL. It is your responsibility to make sure that the array is large enough to hold all the characters read in. Rescue is at hand in the form of fgets() which reads at most n-1 characters from stream, placing them in the array. Should it encounter a new-line character, reading stops and the new-line character is placed in the array. After the characters have been read, a null character is placed in the array.

Comparable functions for writing character strings are:

```
int     puts(const char *string);
int     fputs(const char *string, FILE *stream);
```

puts() writes the contents of the array to which string points to stdout and fputs() writes them to stream. These two functions differ in one important respect: puts() places a new-line character after string but fputs() does not.

The functions gets() and puts() work together in that gets() does not store the new-line character that terminates its input but puts() appends one. In a similar way fgets() and fputs() work together in that fgets() preserves any new-line character and fputs() does not append one.

Program 12.1 can be rewritten as Program 12.2 to read and write strings instead of individual characters. Incidentally it also prompts the user for the names of the source and destination files instead of accepting program arguments. Note, from the sample output, that the prompt for the source file, using puts(), is terminated by new-line whereas the prompt for the destination file, using fputs(), is not. It is however necessary to tell fputs() to place its first argument on stdout. If the length of the response string to the first prompt is zero, stdin is used by assigning this to inputFile. For the destination file, the return value of gets() is used as the first argument to fopen() although its argument, fileName, is used in the error message.

12.5   Formatted Output

Output would be severely limited if all data had to be converted to characters before being output. We need to be able to output integers, real values, characters and strings and at the same time be able to specify the layout of the line on which they will appear. Within this layout we need to be able to indicate how many digits will appear after the decimal point of a real number, how large the field width will be, whether an integer is to be printed in decimal, octal or hexademical.

These facilities, and a few more, are provided by the pair of functions:

```
int     printf(const char *format, ... );
int     fprintf(FILE *stream, const char *format, ... );
```

printf() is equivalent to fprintf() is all respects except that it only writes to stdout.

`format` should point to an array of characters, the contents of which indicate the layout of the output. It may contain conversion specifiers, such as `%d` or `%s`, which specify the format of the subsequent arguments. Any other characters are output as they are. The function may have any number, zero or more, arguments after `format`.

12.5.1 Conversion Specification

The actions of `printf()` are governed by the `format` string. Everything in it is copied to the output except for the conversion specifiers which are replaced by the values of the subsequent arguments. Illustrative output statements are:

```
printf("the answer is %d metres\n", anInteger);
fprintf(dataFile, "date today: %2d %s %4d\n", day, month, year);
printf("Result: %6.1f degrees centigrade\n\n", temperature);
```

which could produce:

```
the answer is 179 metres
date today: 25 December 1879
Result:    78.3 degrees centigrade
```

In the first, the `%d` specifier indicates that the argument `anInteger` has been declared as `int`. In the second, `day` and `year` need to be `int` and `month` needs to be an array of characters. The general form of the conversion specifier is:

```
% flag fieldWidth precision qualifier specifier
```

examples of which are: `%d`, `%i`, `%5i`, `%8.2f`, `%-12.4Le`, `%5.5ld`, `%.3g`. As required, they all start with `%` and then the first and second only have a specifier (`d` and `i`) the third has a field width (`5`) and a specifier (`i`), the fourth a field width (`8`), precision (`.2`) and specifier (`f`), the fifth is the most comprehensive with every component present, namely, a flag (`-`), field width (`12`), precision (`.4`), qualifier (`L`) and a specifier (`e`).

The % and the specifier letter must be present but the other components are optional. The specifier and its qualifier (`h`, `l` or `L`), if present, indicate the type of the corresponding arument and may be one of the following:

Type of argument	Permissible specifiers and qualifiers
char	c
char *	s
short int	hd, hi
unsigned short int	ho, hu, hx, hX
int	d, i
unsigned int	o, u, x, X
long int	ld, li
unsigned long int	lo, lu, lx, lX
double	e, E, f, g, G
long double	Le, LE, Lf, Lg LG

It is your responsibility to ensure that the type of the argument is compatible with the specifier and its qualifier. If it is not, you may obtain unexpected output. For example, if the format string contains a `%d` specifier, `printf()` expects to find a corresponding `int` argument. If your argument happens to be `long int` then you must take care to include the letter l as the qualifier: %ld. It is at this stage that we need to be fully aware that output is not part of the language but is simply managed by library functions. This means that the compiler is unable to check the types of the arguments, apart from those explicitly mentioned in the prototype.

Program 12.3

```
#include <stdio.h>

main()
{
    int       smallInt     =      5;
    int       bigInt       = 8751;
    int       negInt       = -567;
    unsigned  anUnsigned    =   446;
    int       k;

    printf("unsigned specification:   %%o     %%u    %%x     %%X\n");
    printf("%28o    %u   %x    %X\n\n",
                anUnsigned, anUnsigned, anUnsigned, anUnsigned);

    printf("Specifier:    ");
    printf("%%5d    %%-5d     %%-.5d    %%5.3d   %%-5.3d    %%d\n\n");

    for(k = 9; k < 10000; k *= 9)
        printf("             [%5d] [%-5d] [%-.5d] [%5.3d] [%-5.3d] [%d]\n",
                k, k, k, k, k, k);
}
```

Sample output:

```
unsigned specification:    %o      %u      %x      %X
                          676     446     1be     1BE

Specifier:    %5d    %-5d    %-.5d    %5.3d   %-5.3d    %d

            [    9] [9    ] [00009] [   009] [009  ] [9]
            [   81] [81   ] [00081] [   081] [081  ] [81]
            [  729] [729  ] [00729] [   729] [729  ] [729]
            [ 6561] [6561 ] [06561] [  6561] [6561 ] [6561]
```

Where there are different possible specifiers, such as e, f or g for double, each one offers a different style of printed output. These are:

Specifier	Meaning	Sample output
d or i	decimal	12398
o	octal	2370
u	unsigned decimal	12398
x	hexadecimal	34d7f
X	hexadecimal	34D7F
f	form dd.dddddd	123.495
e	form d.dddddde±dd	2.345678e+04
E	form d.ddddddE±dd	2.345678E+04
g or G	uses either f , e or E	
c	character	
s	character string	

Program 12.4

```c
#include   <stdio.h>
#include   <stdlib.h>
#include   <string.h>
#define    maxLine    80

void   printMoney(int    sum);

main()
{
   char    answer[maxLine];

   while(printf("Enter an integer: "), gets(answer) != NULL)
   {
      putchar('£'); printMoney(atoi(answer)); putchar('\n');
   }
}

void printMoney(int sum)
{
   int    right = sum % 1000; /* relative to right-most comma */
   int    left  = sum / 1000;

   if(left > 0)
   {
      printMoney(left);       /* recursive call */
      printf(",%.3d", right); /* leading zeroes */
   }
   else                       /* nothing to left */
      printf("%d", right);    /* no zeroes */
}
```

Sample dialogue (input in bold):

```
Enter an integer: 5↵
£5
Enter an integer: 3856↵
£3,856
Enter an integer: 250008↵
£250,008
Enter an integer: 37000000↵
£37,000,000
```

The specifiers d and i are alternatives for the same type of output. Program 12.3 first illustrates an unsigned integer being output in octal, unsigned and hexadecimal styles. Then is sets out a table of integer values in a range of decimal possibilities:

Specification	Effect
%5d	field width of 5, right justified
%-5d	field width of 5, left justified
%-.5d	precision of 5, left justified
%5.3d	field width of 5, precision of 3
%-5.3d	field width of 5, precision of3, left justified
%d	no field width, use as much space as needed

When printing integer quantities, the precision specifies the minimum number of digits to be displayed and may produce leading zeroes.

Program 12.4 displays integers in monetary form in which each group of three digits is separated by a comma. A recursive function is used; this splits its argument into the two parts, either side of the right-most comma. If there is anything to the left, the right-hand part is displayed as a comma followed by three digits which may include leading zeroes, if needed; if not, no field width is specified.

12.5.2 The Character %

In Program 12.3 we wished to print, in the heading to the table, the character %. Since this has the special meaning of introducing a specifier, we need a mechanism of switching off its special meaning. This is achieved by using % as an escape character; thus %% displays a single %.

12.5.3 Output of Floats and Doubles

The specifiers f and e (or E) offer two styles of output, with the g specifier offering a combination of the two. The L qualifier is used when the argument is long double. float arguments will automatically be converted to double and therefore need no special qualifier.

Program 12.5

```
#include <stdio.h>

main()
{
    double aValue = 1234.123456789;
    double k;

    printf("Specifier        Printed Value\n\n");

    printf(" %%f           [%f]\n",    aValue);
    printf(" %%.2f         [%.2f]\n",  aValue);
    printf(" %%.8f         [%.8f]\n",  aValue);
    printf(" %%.0f         [%.0f]\n",  aValue);
    printf(" %%14.2f       [%14.2f]\n", aValue);
    printf(" %%-14.2f      [%-14.2f]\n", aValue);
    printf(" %%e           [%e]\n",    aValue);
    printf(" %%E           [%E]\n",    aValue);
    printf(" %%.2e         [%.2e]\n",  aValue);
    printf(" %%14.2e       [%14.2e]\n",aValue);
    printf(" %%.0e         [%.0e]\n",  aValue);
    printf(" %%14.0e       [%14.0e]\n",aValue);

    printf("Use of the %%g specifier:\n\n");
    printf("              %%20.12g");
    printf("              %%20.2g                %%20g\n\n");

    for(k = aValue * 1e-10; k < 1e20; k *= 1000)
        printf("%20.12g\t%20.2g\t%20g\n", k, k, k);
}
```

Sample output:

```
Specifier       Printed Value

%f              [1234.123457]
%.2f            [1234.12]
%.8f            [1234.12345679]
%.0f            [1234]
%14.2f          [        1234.12]
%-14.2f         [1234.12        ]
%e              [1.234123e+03]
%E              [1.234123E+03]
%.2e            [1.23e+03]
%14.2e          [      1.23e+03]
%.0e            [1e+03]
%14.0e          [         1e+03]

Use of the %g specifier:

        %20.12g                    %20.2g                    %20g

    1.23412345679e-07            1.2e-07            1.23412e-07
    0.000123412345679            0.00012            0.000123412
      0.123412345679               0.12              0.123412
      123.412345679             1.2e+02               123.412
      123412.345679             1.2e+05                123412
      123412345.679             1.2e+08            1.23412e+08
         123412345679           1.2e+11            1.23412e+11
    1.23412345679e+14           1.2e+14            1.23412e+14
    1.23412345679e+17           1.2e+17            1.23412e+17
```

The value to be printed is rounded to the number of digits of precision specified. The default number of digits displayed after the decimal point is six for the %f and %e specifiers. If a precision of zero is specified then the decimal point is not displayed. Program 12.5 illustrates a variety of formats.

12.5.4 Output of Characters

Characters can be output individually using %c or as strings using %s. For individual characters, all that we can do is to specify the field width. For character strings, the argument must be a pointer to a character which is assumed to be in an array. All characters from there to, but not including, the next ' \0 ' will be used for output. We can arrange for fewer characters to be output. Progam 12.6 illustrates some possibilities.

Program 12.6

```c
#include <stdio.h>

main()
{
    char    letter = 'a';
    char    message[] = "A trial line of output";

    printf("String output:\n");
    printf("%%s             [%s]\n", message);
    printf("%%30s           [%30s]\n", message);
    printf("%%.12s          [%.12s]\n", message);
    printf("%%30.12s        [%30.12s]\n\n", message);

    printf("Sub-string:\n");
    printf("%%.4s           [%.4s]\n", &message[8]);
    printf("%%.7s           [%.7s]\n\n", message + 8);

    printf("Character output:\n");
    printf("%%c             [%c]\n", letter);
    printf("%%5c            [%5c]\n", letter);
}
```

Sample output:

```
String output:
%s          [A trial line of output]
%30s        [      A trial line of output]
%.12s       [A trial line]
%30.12s     [                  A trial line]

Sub-string:
%.4s        [line]
%.7s        [line of]

Character output:
%c          [a]
%5c         [    a]
```

12.6 Formatted Input

The associated activity to formatting the output is that of converting the input sequence of characters into integers, real values and characters strings. This is achieved by the functions:

```
int    scanf(const char *format, ... );
int    fscanf(FILE *stream, const char *format, ... );
```

In the same way that `printf()` writes to `stdout`, `scanf()` reads from `stdin`. `format` points to an array of characters which specifies how the input is to be interpreted. After this come any number of variable arguments i.e. *each must be a pointer to an existing object* since the purpose of each function is to place values into these objects.

Conversion specifiers similar to those used by `printf()` are needed to convert the input stream. The following table sets out which are permissible for each type of argument.

Type of argument	Permissible specifiers
char *	c, s
short int *	hd, hi
unsigned short int *	ho, hu, hx
int *	d, i
unsigned int *	o, u, x
long int *	ld, li
unsigned long int *	lo, lu, lx
float *	e, f, g
double *	le, lf, lg
long double *	Le, Lf, Lg

12.6.1 Input of Numerical Values

The input is viewed as a sequence of characters which needs to be converted into other quantities. With the exception of the `%c` specifier for character conversion, leading white space is skipped. As many characters that will satisfy the specifier are then read.

Program 12.7 accepts an integer and a real value. Two appropriate variables have been created and intialised. For the first set of input data, leading spaces are skipped and the digits `123` are placed into the variable `anInt`. Its associated `%d` specifier accepts digits until it comes across the space immediately following the digit `3`. The `%f` specifier then skips the following spaces and converts the sequence `45.67` into a `float`, placing the value into `aFloat`.

The second set of input data is similar but demonstrates that leading white space can contain new-lines.

The third set contains the sequence `123.456`. The `%d` specifier finds that the first unacceptable character is the point (`.`) leaving this for the next input. The `%f` specifier then accepts the sequence `.456` converting this into a `float` for `aFloat`.

The next two sets of input contain non-digit characters, namely the sequence `answer`. In the first of these sets, the sequence `123` is acceptable as an integer. When the `%f` tries to convert into a `float`, the spaces are skipped but the character 'a' in unacceptable. No value is placed into aFloat, a fact confirmed by the output showing the value to which it was intialised, namely 7.654321. In the final set, the %d specifier comes across the unacceptable character, 'a'. In this case neither anInt nor aFloat have values placed into them.

Program 12.7

```
#include <stdio.h>

main ()
{
    int    anInt  = 987;
    float  aFloat = 7.654321;

    printf("Enter two numbers: ");

    scanf("%d%f", &anInt, &aFloat);
    printf("integer:   %d\n", anInt);
    printf("float:     %f\n", aFloat);
}
```

Sample input (in bold) and output:

```
Enter two numbers:    123    45.67↵
integer:   123
float:     45.669998
```

```
Enter two numbers:↵
↵
   123↵
       45.67↵
integer:   123
float:     45.669998
```

```
Enter two numbers: 123.456↵
integer:   123
float:     0.456000
```

```
Enter two numbers: 123   answer 45.67↵
integer:   123
float:     7.654321
```

```
Enter two numbers:   answer 123 45.67↵
integer:   987
float:     7.654321
```

12.6.2 Value Returned by scanf()

Program 12.7 illustrates the fact that scanf() may not be able to transfer values into all of its arguments. Fortunately, you can discover this from within the program by examining the value returned by scanf(). This is an integer which indicates the number of input items assigned. Program 12.8 is a simple modification which displays this returned value.

Program 12.8

```
#include <stdio.h>

main()
{
    int     anInt  = 987;
    float   aFloat = 7.654321;
    int     returnValue;

    printf("Enter two numbers: ");

    returnValue = scanf("%d%f", &anInt, &aFloat);
    printf("integer:   %d\n", anInt);
    printf("float:     %f\n", aFloat);

    printf("scanf() returned %d\n", returnValue);
}
```

Sample input (in bold) and output:

```
Enter two numbers: 123.45↵
integer:   123
float:     0.450000
scanf() returned 2
```

```
Enter two numbers: 123   answer 45.67↵
integer:   123
float:     7.654321
scanf() returned 1
```

```
Enter two numbers: answer 123 45.67↵
integer:   987
float:     7.654321
scanf() returned 0
```

12.6.3 Input of Character Strings

The %s specifier accepts a sequence of non-white space characters and places them in the array to which the associated argument points. Leading white space is skipped and the conversion stops on the next piece of white space. Program 12.9 demonstrates this effect.

Program 12.9

```c
#include <stdio.h>

#define bufMax    80

main()
{
    char    buffer[bufMax];

    printf("Enter a string: ");
    scanf("%s", buffer);
    printf("String read: [%s]\n", buffer);
}
```

Sample input (in bold) and output:

```
Enter a string: accepts anything up to white space.⏎
String read: [accepts]
```

```
Enter a string: StuffBeforeSpace;:'\(%IsOk  this is not read.⏎
String read: [StuffBeforeSpace;:'\(%IsOk]
```

12.6.4 Input of Characters

To accept an individual character from the input stream, use the %c specifier. This does not skip leading white space but reads the very next character from the input. However, any characters which appear in the format string other than the % specifiers need to match identical characters in the input stream. Any white space, such as a blank, matches any white space in the input stream.

Program 12.10

```c
#include <stdio.h>

main()
{
    char aChar;
    int    int1, int2;
    int returnValue;

    printf("Enter: ");
    returnValue = scanf("%d%c%d", &int1, &aChar, &int2);
    printf("Character selected: [%c]  Items accepted: %d\n",
                                aChar, returnValue);
    printf("Again: ");
    returnValue = scanf("%d %c%d", &int1, &aChar, &int2);
    printf("Character selected: [%c] Items accepted: %d\n",
                                aChar, returnValue);
}
```

Sample input (in bold) and output:

```
Enter: 123p    456↵
Character selected: [p]   Items accepted: 3
Again: 123    p    456↵
Character selected: [p] Items accepted: 3
```

```
Enter: 123   k   456↵
Character selected: [ ]   Items accepted: 2
Again: Character selected: [ ] Items accepted: 0
```

Program 12.10 accepts two integers separated by a character. In the first scanf() the "%d%c%d" format skips any white space before the first integer, accepts the integer, reads the very next character (p), skips any white space and finally reads an integer. In the second scanf(), the "%d %c%d" format skips white space, accepts the integer and then skips white space again, before it reads a character.

When we present to the first scanf() some input which has space between the first integer and the character (p), it accepts a blank as the character but stops when attempting to input the second integer because the stream is then positioned on the 'p'. We have no opportunity to enter another line of data before the second scanf() which also fails because the 'p' is still being offered as the first character of an integer.

12.6.5 Controlling Field Width

When producing output with printf(), we were able to control the field width. In a similar way, we can specify the maximum number of characters which are to be associated with a specifier, e.g. %3d will accept no more than 3 digits into the accompanying integer argument.

Program 12.11 reads lines of digits each of which is intended to represent a date, with the first two digits for the day, the next two for the month and the last four for the year.

Program 12.11

```
#include <stdio.h>

main()
{
    int        d,m,y;
    while(scanf("%2d%2d%4d", &d, &m, &y) != EOF)
        printf("%d/%d/%d\n", d, m, y);
}
```

Sample input:

```
12111992↵
25121991↵
 9121990↵
23 51989↵
```

Sample output:

```
12/11/1992
25/12/1991
91/21/990
23/51/989
```

When we examine the program output, we note that everything seems to be acceptable on the first two lines but not on the others. Leading white space is skipped over: what was intended to be 9/10/1990 becomes 91/21/990 ! The field width of two starts with first character accepted and not at the first character of the line.

Everything is surmountable, even if extra statements are needed:

```
int       d,m,y;
char    buffer[5];

d = atoi(fgets(buffer,3,stdin));
m = atoi(fgets(buffer,3,stdin));
y = atoi(fgets(buffer,5,stdin));

printf("%d/%.2d/%.4d\n", d, m, y);
```

12.7   Internal Transfers

Finally, we examine a pair of functions which do not perform input and output but are closely related to these activities. Instead of converting data values into and from textual form for a file, they carry out the same conversion, under format control, into and from an array of characters:

```
int sprintf(char *buffer, const char *format, ... );
int sscanf(const char *buffer, const char *format, ... );
```

buffer is assumed to point to a character which is the beginning of an array of characters. The functions use the same format conversions as their counterparts, fprintf() and fscanf().

In Chapter 11, when discussing the pre-processor we had the following function which creates a command line to compile a given source file. We build, in the array command, the details which are subsequently issued to the system.

```
void compile(char *source)
{
    char    command[maxSize];
    char    object[maxSize];

    strcpy(object, source);
    *strrchr(object, '.') = '\0';               /* strip the .c */
                              /* place details in array command */
    sprintf(command, "cc -o %s %s", object, source);
    system(command);                        /* issue the command */
}
```

The function `scanf()` which accepts formatted input, sometimes causes problems which can be overcome with judicious use of `sscanf()`. Suppose we are inviting the user to enter two integer values which are to refer to an element in a matrix by row and column:

```
int     row;
int     col;

printf("Enter the row and column: ");
scanf("%d%d", &row, &column);
process(row, col);
```

This works well until the user fails to read the prompt correctly and only enters one value. Nothing happens; the user is puzzled. We would like to be able to deduce that he has entered only one value and remind him to enter the second:

```
if(scanf("%d%d", &row, &column) == 2)
    process(row, column);
else
    printf("Please enter two values\n");
```

Unfortunately, this does not work. After the user has entered one value, `scanf()` is skipping white space, looking for another integer.

We need to read, with `gets()`, the complete line that the user has entered and examine it with `sscanf()`:

```
char    theLine[maxLine];

printf("Enter the row and column: ");
gets(theLine);
if(sscanf(theLine, "%d%d", &row, &column) == 2)
    process(row, column);
else
    printf("Please enter two values\n");
```

or preferably:

```
while(gets(theLine), sscanf(theLine, "%d%d", &row, &column) < 2)
    printf("Please enter two values\n");

process(row, column);
```

or possibly:

```
while(sscanf(gets(theLine), "%d%d", &row, &column) < 2)
    printf("Please enter two values\n");

process(row, column);
```

12.8 Unformatted Input and Output

When we are storing data on a file for later use by a program, it is unnecessary, to format them. Formatting is simply a way of making data intelligible to the human eye. The contents of data variables can be written to and/or read from a file without conversion by the two functions:

```
size_t fread(void *ptr, size_t size, size_t n, FILE *stream);

size_t fwrite(const void *ptr, size_t size, size_t n, FILE *stream);
```

The type `size_t` is defined in the header file `stddef.h` as the unsigned integral type which the operator `sizeof` produces. It will typically be `typedef`ed to represent `unsigned int`.

Program 12.12

```
#include <stdio.h>
#include <stdlib.h>

typedef someType Info;              /* someType needs to be replaced
                                       by any specific type */
#define    maxDetails    120

main()
{
    Info    details[maxDetails], someInformation;
    FILE    *detailsFile;
    char    *fileName = "detail.file";
    int     k;

    if((detailsFile = fopen(fileName, "w")) == NULL)
        exit(1);

            /* put data into the array details and into someInformation */

                    /* output the contents of the array details */
    fwrite(details, sizeof(details[0]), maxDetails, detailsFile);

                    /* an alternative way to output the array */
    fwrite(details, sizeof(details), 1, detailsFile);

                    /* output the contents of the k th element */
    fwrite(details + k, sizeof(details[0]), 1, detailsFile);

                    /* an alternative way to output one element */
    fwrite(&details[k], sizeof(details[0]), 1, detailsFile);

                    /* output the content of someInformation */
    fwrite(&someInformation, sizeof(someInformation), 1 detailsFile);

    fclose(detailsFile);
}
```

`fread()` transfers n items of data, each of `size` bytes, from `stream` and place them in memory, starting at the location to which `ptr` points.

`fwrite()` works in a similar manner but transfers data in the opposite direction. Notice that `ptr` is declared to be a pointer to a constant thus ensuring that the function will not alter the contents to which `ptr` points.

Program 12.12 illustrates the use of `fwrite()`. `Info` is an alternative name for some specific type which could be a structure, an array or a simple type. The `main()` function declares an array `details` of type `Info` and a single quantity, `someInformation`. After the file `detailsFile` has been opened successfully, the full contents of the array `details` are written; two ways of doing this are shown. It is possible to write `maxDetails` elements, each the size of an individual element (`sizeof(details[0])`) or to write them as one item whose size is that of the array (`sizeof(details)`).

Next, two ways of writing an individual element of the array are shown; the only difference between them is in the way in which the address of the element is written. Finally, the contents of `someInformation` are written.

`fwrite()` returns a value: the number of items successfully transmitted. To be completely safe, we should write:

```
numberWritten = fwrite(details, sizeof(details[0]),
                       maxDetails, detailsFile);
if(numberWritten <maxDetails)
    fprintf(stderr, "write error: insufficient items written");
```

`fread()` is used in a similar way; it returns the number of items successfully read; comparable statements would be:

```
fread(details, sizeof(details[0]), maxDetails, detailsFile);

fread(details, sizeof(details), 1, detailsFile);

fread(details + k, sizeof(details[0]), 1, detailsFile);

fread(&details[k], sizeof(details[0]), 1, detailsFile);

fread(&someInformation, sizeof(someInformation), 1 detailsFile);

numberRead = fread(details, sizeof(details[0]),
                   maxDetails, detailsFile);
if(numberRead <maxDetails)
    fprintf(stderr, "read error: insufficient items read");
```

12.8.1 Positioning the File Pointer

In Program 12.15 successive calls to `fwrite()` caused new data to be added to the end of the file. A position indicator into the file is maintained and can be changed so that the next call to `fwrite()`, or to `fread()`, can transfer data to/from any point in the file. The language imposes no structure on a file, simply regarding it as a consecutive sequence of bytes.

The following function is used to position this indicator:

```
int fseek(FILE *stream, long offset, int place);
```

the position indicator of the stream is placed offset bytes according to constants defined in the header file stdio.h:

place	new position relative to:
SEEK_SET	beginning of the file
SEEK_CUR	current position
SEEK_END	end of the file

Typical uses of this function are:

```
                                   /* move to beginning of file */
fseek(detailsFile, 0, SEEK_SET);

                                     /* move forward one item */
fseek(detailsFile, sizeof(details[0]), SEEK_CUR);

                                      /* move back one item */
fseek(detailsFile, -sizeof(details[0]), SEEK_CUR);

                                     /* move to end of file */
fseek(detailsFile, 0, SEEK_END);

                            /* move to k items before the end of file */
fseek(detailsFile, -k * sizeof(details[0]), SEEK_END);
```

If fseek() is unable to position the indicator as required, it returns a non-zero value otherwise is returns zero. For example, attempting to position the indicator before the start of the file would result in a non-zero value being returned.

The current position of the indicator can be obtained by:

```
long ftell(FILE *stream);
```

which returns the offset in bytes from the start of the file. With this, we can note the current position so that we can return to it at a later stage:

```
long    position;
                                   /* note the current position */
position = ftell(detailsFile);

/* carry out other processing on the file */

                                   /* return to the earlier position */
fseek(detailsFile, position, SEEK_SET);
```

One limitation with ftell() is that is only returns a long int. This is acceptable if the file does not contain more bytes than the maximum value of a long int. To overcome this problem, two more functions are provided:

```
int fgetpos(FILE *stream, fpos_t *position);
```

```
int fsetpos(FILE *stream, const fpos_t *position);
```

fpos_t is defined in `stdio.h`. `fgetpos()` notes the current position in the object to which `position` points. The information contained in it is intended only for use by a subsequent call to `fsetpos()`. In fact the value given to `fsetpos()` by `position` *must have been obtained by a prior call* to `fgetpos()`.

```
fpos_t curentPosition;
                                    /* note the current position */
fgetpos(detailsFile, &currentPosition);

/* carry out other processing on the file */
                                    /* return to the earlier position */
fsetpos(detailsFile, &currentPosition);
```

Each function returns zero is it was successful and non-zero if not.

13

Standard Library

We have noted that C is a small, compact and efficient language which would be diminished in value if there did not exist an extensive library of functions. In addition to standardising the language itself the ANSI Standard specifies what should be in the standard library and how each function should perform.

Chapter 9 paid particular attention to functions which handle character strings and Chapter 12 concerned itself with functions for input and output. In this chapter we list most of the functions in the standard library with a brief description of each. In practice, you should consult the reference manual for the compiler you are using.

13.1 Header Files

The functions in the library are arranged into logical groups each of which has an associated header file which contains prototypes for all the functions in that group plus some definitions. The full set of header files is:

assert.h	locale.h	stddef.h
ctype.h	math.h	stdio.h
errno.h	setjmp.h	stdlib.h
float.h	signal.h	string.h
limits.h	stdargs.h	time.h

The headers float.h, limits.h and stddef.h contain no prototypes but simply constants. Use of the first two were illustrated in Program 4.1 of chapter 4. stddef.h defines quantities such as size_t.

13.2   Handling Errors

Header file: `errno.h`

Many functions set an error condition if they fail to carry out their task correctly. A global integer quantity `errno` is then set to a non-zero value. This can be examined and reported:

```
#include <stdio.h>

void   perror(const char *string);
```

This prints a message relating to the current value of `errno`, prefixed by the contents of `string`. Program 13.1 illustrates possible error messages.

Program 13.1

```
#include <stdio.h>
#include <errno.h>

main()
{
   char   message[80];

   for(errno = 1; errno < 35; errno++)
   {
      sprintf(message, "Error no: %5i ", errno);
      perror(message);
   }
}
```

Sample abbreviated output:

```
Error no:      1 : Permission denied
Error no:      2 : No such file or directory
Error no:      3 : No such resource
Error no:      4 : Interrupted system service
Error no:      5 : I/O error
Error no:      6 : No such device or address
Error no:      7 : Argument list too long
Error no:      8 : Exec format error
...
Error no:     29 : Illegal seek
Error no:     30 : Read-only file system
Error no:     31 : Too many links
Error no:     32 : Broken pipe
Error no:     33 : Math arg out of domain of func
Error no:     34 : Math result not representable
```

13.3   Character Handling

Header file: `ctype.h`

Each of the followings test whether a given character, aChar, is a particular type of character, such as upper case (`isupper()`). Each function returns *true* or *false* in the form of an integer.

```
int     isalnum(int aChar);          /* letter or digit */
int     isalpha(int aChar);          /* letter */
int     iscntrl(int aChar);          /* control character */
int     isdigit(int aChar);          /* digit */
int     isgraph(int aChar);          /* any printing character
                                        except space */
int     islower(int aChar);          /* lower case */
int     isprint(int aChar);          /* any printing character
                                        including space */
int     ispunct(int aChar);          /* any printing character
                                        except space, letter or
                                        digit */
int     isspace(int aChar);          /* any white space */
int     isupper(int aChar);          /* upper case */
int     isxdigit(int aChar);         /* hexadecimal digit */
```

Converting case: the following two functions return the upper case or lower case equivalent of the argument. If it makes no sense to make this conversion, e.g. to find the upper case of 'G' or the lower case of ']', each function returns the character unconverted:

```
int     tolower(int aChar);
int     toupper(int aChar);
```

13.4   Mathematical Functions

Header file: `math.h`

13.4.1 Trigonometric Functions:

```
double cos(double x);                /* cosine in radians */
double sin(double x);                /* sine in radians */
double tan(double x);                /* tangent in radians */
```

13.4.2 Inverse Trigonometric Functions:

```
double acos(double x);               /* arc cosine - principal value */
double asin(double x);               /* arc sine - principal value */
double atan(double x);               /* arc tangent - principal value */
```

```
double atan2(double x, double y));/* principal value of y/x, using
                                     signs of both to determine the
                                     quadrant */
```

13.4.3 Hyperbolic Functions:

```
double cosh(double x);                /* hyperbolic cosine */
double sinh(double x);                /* hyperbolic sine */
double tanh(double x);                /* hyperbolic tangent */
```

13.4.4 Exponential and Logarithmic Functions

```
double exp(double x); /* exponential */
double log(double x); /* natural logarithm */
double log10(double x);/* logarithm to base 10 */

double fexp(double aValue, int *exponent);
            /* scales aValue by powers of 2, returning the
               magnitude in range 0.5 to 1 and the power of 2 in
               *exponent */

double ldexp(double x, int exponent);
            /* reverse of fexp() - multiplies x by 2 raised to
               power exponent */

double modf(double value, double *fraction);
            /* breaks value into integral and fractional parts */
```

Use of these last three functions is illustrated in Program 13.2.

Program 13.2   (illustrating frexp(), ldexp() and modf())

```c
#include <stdio.h>
#include <math.h>

main()
{
    int          exponent;
    double       value;
    long double  integralPart;
    double       result;

    printf("    frexp():                           ldexp():\n");
    printf("    argument      returned     power\n");
    printf("                   value       of 2\n");
    for(value = 123e-5; value < 1e5; value *= 10)
    {
        result = frexp(value, &exponent);
        printf("%10.2e %10.3f  %9i", value, result, exponent);
        result = ldexp(result, exponent);
        printf("%15.2e\n", result);
    }

    printf("\n    modf():\n");
    printf("    argument    whole part    fraction\n");
    for(value = -123e-5; fabs(value) < 1e5; value *= -10)
```

```
    {
        result = modf(value, &integralPart);
        printf("%10.2e    %10.2e    %10.2e\n",
                  value, integralPart, result);
    }
}
```

Sample output:

frexp(): argument	returned value	power of 2	ldexp():
1.23e-03	0.630	-9	1.23e-03
1.23e-02	0.787	-6	1.23e-02
1.23e-01	0.984	-3	1.23e-01
1.23e+00	0.615	1	1.23e+00
1.23e+01	0.769	4	1.23e+01
1.23e+02	0.961	7	1.23e+02
1.23e+03	0.601	11	1.23e+03
1.23e+04	0.751	14	1.23e+04

modf(): argument	whole part	fraction
-1.23e-03	-0.00e+00	-1.23e-03
1.23e-02	0.00e+00	1.23e-02
-1.23e-01	-0.00e+00	-1.23e-01
1.23e+00	1.00e+00	2.30e-01
-1.23e+01	-1.20e+01	-3.00e-01
1.23e+02	1.23e+02	0.00e+00
-1.23e+03	-1.23e+03	-0.00e+00
1.23e+04	1.23e+04	0.00e+00

13.4.5 Miscellaneous

```
    double ceil(double x);                  /* smallest integer above x */
    double floor(double x);                 /* largest integer below x */
    double fabs(double x);                  /* absolute value of x */
    double fmod(double x, double y);        /* remainder of x/y */
    double pow(double x, double y);         /* x raised to power y */
    double sqrt(double x);                  /* square root of x */
```

13.5   Input and Output

Chapter 12 discusses the collection of input and output functions. They are grouped here for reference.

Header file: **stdio.h**

13.5.1 Operations on files

```
    int    remove(const char *filename); /* remove file from system */
```

```
int     rename(const char *old, const char *new);
                            /* change old name to new name */

FILE    *tempfile(void);          /* create a temporary file */
```

13.5.2 Access Functions

```
int     fopen(const char *filename, const char *mode);
                            /* open filename in given mode */

int     fclose(FILE *stream);     /* close stream */

int     freopen(const char *filename, const char *mode, FILE *stream);
                            /* close stream and re-use it for
                               filename in given mode */

int     fflush(FILE *stream);     /* for an output file, send all
                               unwritten data to the file */

int     setvbuf(FILE *stream, char *buf, int mode, size_t size);
                            /* sets up a buffer, pointed to by
                               buf and of given size;
                               arranges form of buffering
                               according to mode:
                                 _IOFBF fully buffered
                                 _IOLBF line buffered
                                 _IONBF unbuffered */
```

13.5.3 Character and String Handling

```
int     getchar(void);            /* character from stdin */

int     getc(FILE *stream);       /* character from stream */

int     fgetc(FILE *stream);      /* function equivalent of
                               getc() */

char    *gets(char *aString);     /* aString from stdin */

char    *fgets(char *aString, int n, FILE *stream);
                            /* aString from stream */

int     putchar(int aChar);       /* aChar to stdout */

int     putc(int aChar, FILE *stream);/* aChar to stream */

int     fputc(int aChar, FILE *stream); /* function equivalent of
                               putc() */

int     puts(const char *aString);   /* aString to stdout */

int     fputs(const char *aString, FILE *stream);
                            /* aString to stream */

int     ungetc(int aChar, FILE *stream);/* put aChar back on stream */
```

13.5.4 Formatted Input and Output

```
int     fprintf(FILE *stream, const char *format, ... );

int     printf(const char *format, ... );/* fprintf() to stdout */

int     sprintf(char *string, FILE *stream, const char *format, ... );
                                        /* output to string */

int     fscanf(FILE *stream, const char *format, ... );

int     scanf(const char *format, ... );  /* fscanf() from stdin */

int     sscanf(const char *string, FILE *stream,
               const char *format,..);
                                    /* input from string */
```

13.5.5 Unformatted Input and Output

```
size_t fread(void *ptr, size_t size, size_t n, FILE *stream);

size_t fwrite(const void *ptr, size_t size, size_t n, FILE *stream);
```

13.5.6 File Positioning

```
int     fgetpos(FILE *stream, fpos_t *position);
                                    /* obtain current position */

int     fsetpos(FILE *stream, const fpos_t *position);
                                    /* set position */

int     fseek(FILE *stream, long offset, int place);
                                    /* set file position to offset
                                       according to place:
                                       SEEK_SET start of file
                                       SEEK_CUR current position
                                       SEEK_END end of file */

long    ftell(FILE *stream);        /* obtain current position */

void    rewind(FILE *stream);       /* equivalent to
                                       fseek(stream, 0, SEEK_SET); */
```

13.5.7 Error Handling

```
void    clearerr(FILE *stream);     /* clears end of file and
                                       error indicators for stream */

int     feof(FILE *stream);         /* tests end of file indicator
                                       on stream */
```

```
int     ferror(FILE *stream);        /* tests error indicator on
                                         stream */

void    perror(const char *aString); /* prints error message of
                                         current value of errno,
                                         preceded by aString */
```

13.6   General Utilities

Header file: **stdlib.h**

13.6.1 String Conversion Functions

Each of the following three functions converts the contents of aString to a numerical value, skipping leading white space; a pointer to the remaining part of the aString is placed, by the function, in restOfString. For the functions returning integral values, the base of the number can be specified:

```
double strtod(const char *aString, char **restOfString);
long   strtol(const char *aString, char **restOfString, int base);
unsigned long strtoul(const char *aString, char **restOfString,
                                                       int base);
```

The next three functions are simplified equivalents of the above and have been kept in the Standard for earlier programs:

```
double atof(const char *aString);
int    atoi(const char *aString);
long   atol(const char *aString);
```

13.6.2 Pseudo-random Number Generation

```
int     rand(void);                  /* returns pseudo-random
                                         number in range 0 to
                                         RAND_MAX */
void    srand(unsigned int seed);    /* set the starting point of
                                         the sequence to seed */
```

13.7   Memory Management

Header file: **stdlib.h**

```
void    *malloc(size_t n);           /* allocate n bytes of storage */

void    *calloc(size_t nItems, size_t n);
                                     /* allocate nItems of storage
                                         each of n bytes,
                                         initialised to zero */
```

```
void    *realloc(void *memory, size_t n);
                                         /* re-allocate storage pointed
                                            to by memory and make is
                                            n bytes */

void    free(void *memory);              /* de-allocate storage pointed
                                            to by memory */
```

13.8   Communicating with the Environment

Header file: stdlib.h

```
void    exit(int status);                /* normal termination and
                                            return to operating system
                                            with the value of status:
                                                EXIT_SUCCESS
                                                EXIT_FAILURE */

void    abort(void);                     /* abnormal termination;
                                            equivalent to
                                                raise(SIGABRT) */

int     atexit(void (*function)(void))   /* on normal termination,
                                            execute function */

char    *getenv(const char *name);       /* obtain environment string
                                            for given name */

int     system(const char *aString);     /* issue aString to the
                                            operating system */
```

13.9   Searching and Sorting

Header file: stdlib.h

Each of the next two functions considers anArray, containing nItems elements each of size sizeOfItem. Each needs to be provided with a comparison function compare().

```
void    qsort(void *anArray, size_t nItems, size_t sizeOfItem,
                  int (*compare)(const void *, const void *));

                     /* sorts the anArray, the arguments of
                        compare() are items in anArray */
```

```
void    *bsearch(const void *key, const void *anArray, size_t nItems,
                 size_t sizeOfItem,
                 int (*compare)(const void *, const void*)));

                        /* searches anArray using compare() whose
                           first argument points to the key object
                           and second argument points to an item in
                           anArray */
```

13.10   Integer Arithmetic Functions

Header file: `stdlib.h`

```
int     abs(int aValue);            /* absolute value of aValue */
long    labs(long aValue);          /* long int equivalent */
```

Each of the following divides `numerator` by `denominator` and returns the quotient and remainder in a structure:

```
typedef struct {
                int quot;           /* quotient */
                int rem;            /* remainder */
              }
                div_t;

div_t  div(int numerator, int denominator);

                          /* long int equivalent */
ldiv_t ldiv(long numerator, long denominator);
```

13.11   String Handling

Header file: `string.h`

The functions in this section fall into three groups, indicated by their initial letters; each group handles a different sequences of bytes:

initial letters	type of sequence
str	null terminated strings
strn	null terminated strings of maximum length
mem	sequences of specified length

13.11.1   Copying

```
void    *memcpy(void *destination, const void *source, size_t n);
void    *memmove(void *destination, const void *source, size_t n);
char    *strcpy(char *destination, const char *source);
char    *strncpy(char *destination, const char *source, size_t n);
```

`memcpy()` does not handle overlapping sequences whereas `memmove()` does

13.11.2   Concatenation
```
char   *strcat(char *destination, const char *source);
char   *strncat(char *destination, const char *source, size_t n);
```

Each appends source to destination.

13.11.3   Comparison
```
int    memcmp(const void *s1, const void *s2, size_t n);
int    strcmp(const char *s1, const char *s2);
int    strncmp(const char *s1, const char *s2, size_t n);
```

Returned value is:

negative	s1 before s2
zero	s1 same as s2
positive	s1 after s2

13.11.4   Character Search
```
void   *memchr(const void *sequence, int aChar, size_t n);
                        /* finds left-most aChar in sequence */

char   *strchr(const char *aString, int aChar);
                        /* finds left-most aChar in aString */

char   *strrchr(const char *aString, int aChar);
                        /* finds right-most aChar in aString */

char   *strstr(const char *s1, const char *s2);
                        /* finds left-most occurrence of s2 in s1 */

char   *strpbrk(const char *s1, const char *s2);
                        /* finds left-most occurrence in s1 of
                           any character from s2 */

size_t strspn(const char *s1, const char *s2);
                        /* finds length of substring of s1
                           containing only characters in s2 */

size_t strcspn(const char *s1, const char *s2);
                        /* complement of strspn: finds length of
                           substring of s1 not containing
                           characters in s2 */

char   *strtok(char *s1, const char *s2);
                        /* breaks s1 into a sequence of tokens,
                           each delimited by a character from s2
                           */
```

13.11.5   Miscellaneous
```
size_t strlen(const char *aString);
                        /* finds length of aString */

void   *memset(void *sequence, int aChar, size_t n);
```

```
                         /* copies aChar into the first n
                            characters of sequence */

char    *strerror(int errorNumber);
                         /* returns a pointer to the error message
                            associated with errorNumber */
```

13.12   Date and Time

Header file: **time.h**

The header file defines two types which are typically:

```
typedef unsigned long int clock_t;
typedef unsigned long int time_t;
```

a constant which is typically:

```
#define CLOCKS_PER_SEC 60
```

and a structure which is:

```
struct tm {
    int tm_sec;        /* Seconds after the minute -- [0, 61] */
    int tm_min;        /* Minutes after the hour -- [0, 59] */
    int tm_hour;       /* Hours after midnight -- [0, 23] */
    int tm_mday;       /* Day of the month -- [1, 31] */
    int tm_mon;        /* Months since January -- [0, 11] */
    int tm_year;       /* Years since 1900 */
    int tm_wday;       /* Days since Sunday    [0, 6] */
    int tm_yday;       /* Days since January 1 -- [0, 365] */
    int tm_isdst;      /* Daylight Savings Time flag */
};


clock_t    clock(void);
                         /* returns processor times since start of
                            execution: convert to seconds by
                            dividing by  CLOCKS_PER_SEC */

double     difftime(time_t time1, time_t time0);
                         /* computes time1 - time0 as seconds */

time_t     time(time_t *timer);
                         /* returns the current calendar time and
                            assigns this to *timer */

char       *asctime(const struct tm *timePointer);
                         /* converts a time in the structure to
                            which timePointer points to a string
                            of the form:
                            Tue Apr 12 03:43:18 1993\n\0 */

struct tm *localtime(const time_t *timer);
                         /* converts calendar time, pointed to by
                            timer to structured local time */
```

```
char        *ctime(const time_t *timer);
                      /* converts a calendar time pointed to by
                         timer to a string; equivalent to
                         asctime(localtime(timer)); */

struct tm *gmtime(const time_t *timer);
                      /* converts calendar time pointed to by
                         timer to structured Greenwich Mean
                         Time */
```

13.13   Signals

Header file: **signal.h**

When unusual situations, called *signals*, occur it is possible to write a function, called a signal handler, in which you control the actions to be taken. The header file defines a number of constants which represent the possible signals. Typical of these are:

signal	meaning
SIGABRT	abnormal termination, initiated by abort()
SIGFPE	floating point exception, such as division by zero
SIGILL	illegal instruction
SIGINT	interrupt by user
SIGSEGV	invalid access to storage; segmentation violation

The following function enables us to indicate what action to take when a particular signal arises:

```
void    (*signal(int aSignal, void (*aFunction)(int)))(int);
```

This complicated prototype says that signal() is a function which takes two arguments: an integer signal number, aSignal, and a pointer to a function, aFuntion, which itself takes an integer argument. signal() returns a pointer to the value of aFunction for the most recent call to signal() for the specified signal, aSignal.

This can be helped by judicious use of typedef:

```
typedef    void   intFunc(int);
intFunc    (*signal)(int, intFunc *);
```

where intFunc is a function which takes an int argument and returns void; signal is then a function, taking and int and a pointer to intFunc as arguments and returning a pointer to intFunc. With the aid of one more typedef we can write:

```
typedef        void      intFunc(int);
typedef        intFunc   *ptrIntFunc;
ptrIntFunc     signal(int, ptrIntFunc);
```

Here, ptrIntfunc is a pointer to an intFunc; signal is a function taking an int and a ptrIntFunc as arguments and returning a ptrIntFunc.

Signals are raised by the various situations mentioned above but can also be raised deliberately which can be useful when testing programs:

```
int     raise(int aSignal);
```

Program 13.3 illustrates the use of some signals. The function myHandler() provides special, simple actions when a signal arises. When this happens, the default action is restored and so the first action of the function is to restore this handler. It then detects which signal has arisen and displays an appropriate message.

In the main() function, myHandler() is set to be the handler for floating point exception (SIGFPE) and illegal instruction (SIGILL). For other signals, the default action takes place. A second function, interrupt(), is set up as the action when an interrupt (SIGINT) occurs.

The main() function also indicates that when the program exits, the function exitFunction() is activated. This is achieved by using the library function atexit() which is detailed in section 13.9.

Program 13.3
_____

```
#include <stdio.h>
#include <signal.h>
#include <stdlib.h>

void    myHandler(int aSignal)
{
    signal(aSignal, myHandler);    /* reset this signal handler */
    printf("myHandler: ");
    switch(aSignal)
    {
        case SIGFPE: printf("Floating point exception\n");
                     break;
        case SIGILL: printf("Illegal instruction\n");
                     break;
        default:     printf("does not handle signal %d\n");
                     break;
    }
}

void    interrupt(int aSignal)
{
    printf("Interrupted\n");
    exit(EXIT_FAILURE);
}

void    exitFunction()
{
    printf("My exit function\n");
}
```

```
main()
{
    signal(SIGFPE, myHandler);
    signal(SIGILL, myHandler);
    signal(SIGINT, interrupt);
    atexit(exitFunction);

    printf("In main() before raising floating point exception\n");
    raise(SIGFPE);
    printf("back in main(), about to raise illegal instruction\n");
    raise(SIGILL);
    printf("back in main() again\n");

    printf("stop by interrupting\n");
    for(;;)
    {
        printf("repetitive output\n");
    }

    printf("This should never appear\n");
}
```

Sample output:

```
In main() before raising floating point exception
myHandler: Floating point exception
back in main(), about to raise illegal instruction
myHandler: Illegal instruction
back in main() again
stop by interrupting
repetitive output
repetitive output
repetitive output
repetitive output
...
repetitive output
repetitive output
repetitive output
Interrupted
My exit function
```

The default action for a signal can be re-instated by:

```
signal(SIGFPE, SIG_DFL);        /* restore default for floating
                                   point exception */
```

or a signal can be ignored by:

```
signal(SIGINT, SIG_IGN);        /* ignore interrupt signals */
```

Index